SAMS

SIMPLIFIED ASSET MANAGEMENT SYSTEMS

PYOTR STILOVSKY

AuthorHouse™ UK
1663 Liberty Drive
Bloomington, IN 47403 USA
www.authorhouse.co.uk
UK TFN: 0800 0148641 (Toll Free inside the UK)
UK Local: 02036 956322 (+44 20 3695 6322 from outside the UK)

Because of the dynamic nature of the Internet, any web addresses or links contained in this book may have changed
since publication and may no longer be valid. The views expressed in this work are solely those of the author and do not
necessarily reflect the views of the publisher, and the publisher hereby disclaims any responsibility for them.

Any people depicted in stock imagery provided by Getty Images are models,
and such images are being used for illustrative purposes only.
Certain stock imagery © Getty Images.

This book is printed on acid-free paper.

ISBN: 978-1-6655-8268-1 (sc)
ISBN: 978-1-6655-8267-4 (e)

Print information available on the last page.

Published by AuthorHouse 11/30/2020

authorHOUSE

Contents

Abbreviations

AL	Asset life
AM	Asset management
AMP	Asset management plan
AMS	Asset management system
BSI	British Standards Institution
CAV	Current asset value
CCTV	Closed circuit television
DMA	District meter area
d/s	Downstream
DCF	Discounted cash flow
CG	Condition grade
CIP	Capital investment programme
CMMS	Computerized maintenance management system
GRAMS	Generic asset management system
IAM	Institute of Asset Management
LoS	Levels of service
M&E	Mechanical and electrical
MEAV	Modern equivalent asset value
NVQ	National vocational qualification
OFWAT	Office of Water Regulation
OS	Ordnance Survey
PAS	Publicly available specification
PG	Performance grade
PoP	Plant or pipeline
PWS	My initials
RAL	Remaining asset life
SAMS	Simplified asset management system
SDA	Specific drainage area
TOTEX	Total asset life expenditure
TRAMP	Trinidad asset management plan
u/s	Upstream
USD ($)	US dollar
WHO	World Health Organization
WRc	Water Research Centre

There are others in the more detailed papers but they should be self explanatory.

Foreword

"Why have an Asset Management Plan?

Asset Management Planning improves the management and maintenance of essential assets in businesses and the utilities sector whilst increasing the effectiveness of management. It improves equipment reliability whilst maximising efficiency and output. This in turn helps to reduce unexpected large maintenance or replacement costs and avoids inconvenient outages caused by ageing infrastructure. A plan, based on a sound Asset Management System, will improve customer service and increase the organisation's return on its investments.

Being a civil engineer I have been involved in the creation of new assets since I started work on Manchester's slum clearance program in 1964. In 1975 I moved from local government to the water industry. However, it was not until 1996, when I took early retirement from the core business of Severn Trent Water, and moved full-time to international work, that I came across 'asset management' as a subject in its own right. I had been asked to produce an 'asset management plan' for the water services in Trinidad and Tobago and use cost-effective IT services in doing it. I spent six months there working on the AMP as well as a water resources strategy for the country. Along with local staff, I was able to co-author two papers on the subject which were presented to the Caribbean Water Conference in 1997 and 1998. In Trinidad we called the system 'TRAMP' (work it out for yourself).

Subsequently, I introduced AM into a number of countries, always as part of a very time-limited and cost effective exercise. To simplify things, I set out a series of steps which come in a logical order and hence the title of this book – _Simplified_ _Asset Management Systems_. Along the way I produced numerous papers, procedures and presentations which I have made available on-line as a 'knowledge sharing' exercise:

http://felixschrodinger.wordpress.com/category/asset-management/

In undertaking these tasks, I noticed a great disparity in the understanding of AM, from the smallest, meanest localized system to the heavyweights of PAS 55 and ISO 55000 et al. However, my most relevant observation is to call into question those systems which rely solely on asset lives and condition as their basis for valuation and prioritization. In Jordan I was shown a copy of the plan for a large Scottish city which had been produced by consultants at great expense. It was the most elegant and complex spreadsheet I have ever seen. However, it had been compiled by an IT expert working with an accountant so the essential asset lives were simply based on the 'straight-line depreciation curve' which we all know.

Systems such as these have lost all contact with the 'customer' who, in the long run is the one who matters most. You might not know how to define 'performance grades' (yet) but, without them, the whole point of the exercise is lost. Even the UK's water regulator confuses condition and performance in its official advice to water companies.

With any subject like this, a few diagrams and tables are necessary to promote clarity. However, when perusing the internet you will come across a myriad of conflicting illustrations, most of which have been produced by what we used to call 'the department of clever diagrams'.

The term 'asset management planning' is the set of actions required to carry out the function of 'asset management' and should result in an 'asset management plan' (AMP). The asset management system' (AMS) is the set-up which runs things. They are often confused without too much bother.

There is quite a bit of duplication in the content herein. This is because of the way that I produced the papers which have been compiled (some would say cobbled) together to make up a complete coverage of the subject. Apologies for that though some would say that repetition is no bad thing and it does give a flavour of how things can be adapted to different scenarios.

Thanks to Alan Sutton and Wayne Earp for comments on the draft manuscript and to Jay Uno for the cover photograph.

Background

Following publication of a number of damning papers and articles, the state of the nation's sewers became a hot topic in the late 1970s and investigations were undertaken to determine the scale of the problem. As an aid to ranking the condition of individual pipelines, WRc produced *The Sewerage Rehabilitation Manual* and appended a wall chart of CCTV stills indicating typical conditions of gravity sewers. These were ranked and, over time, became the accepted 1-5 grading system that most asset managers use today.

Following these beginnings, asset management (AM) was pioneered in New Zealand and Australia in the 1980s and has been adopted by a number of businesses in the UK. In particular it has featured heavily in OFWAT's regulation of the water industry in England and Wales where systems were standardized and methodologies refined. These practices and procedures have been used in many countries across the world enabling water (and other) undertakings to produce investment programs to look after their assets in the longer term. Whilst some have access to standards for compiling an AMS in their industry or country, many do not, hence this book seeks to address that problem by providing advice on how to build a system from scratch. The IAM and BSI will hate it and be assured, this book is approved by neither of them. Whilst many of the basics relate to water industry assets there are also models for highways and social housing which serve as examples and can be developed further.

What you need:

- The commitment of management to develop a system
- The co-operation of other departments enabling access to sites and data collection
- A small team with the right mentality who are committed to carry out the work
- One or two PCs and basic office software
- A digital camera, a high-viz jacket and basic understanding of H&S requirements
- Time and funding to carry out the necessary development and survey work

An A3 colour printer is useful for printing out large spreadsheets.

What you don't need:

- ISO 55000 or PAS 55
- Membership of the IAM
- Expensive consultants
- Complex or proprietary software
- A degree in engineering
- A silo mentality

The chapters which follow are in a logical order which will enable the team to build a robust system without excessive effort or expense. The basic procedure is simply this:

- Compile a list of assets in a spreadsheet or database
- Grade them for condition
- Compile levels of service criteria
- Grade the assets for performance
- Add replacement costs
- Carry out valuation
- Compile outputs for the capital investment program and strategies
- Calculate necessary future investment required to replace assets as they wear out

Introduction

Asset management can mean different things to different people. If you Google it, you will find many finance managers trying to sell you their services in order to manage your finances, especially stocks and shares; this is 'financial' asset management. There also many who use the term, especially in the field of IT, to 'manage' portable assets such as laptop computers in order to know who has them, where they are located, and what software is mounted on them. Fleet managers are known to use similar systems to keep tabs on the vehicles in their care.

However, none of this is pertinent to SAMS - here, we are talking about 'infrastructure' asset management and all that that implies. It is a series of related systems, practices and procedures which enable us to keep tabs on our company's assets in order to ensure that they continue to perform the required tasks, thus enabling the company to deliver its services to its customers. It can be adapted to include any physical asset but is mostly applied to infrastructure whether static, transportable or mobile. You could apply all of this to your own home.

A short perusal on-line will help you gain some insight into the jargon but, generally, will not enlighten you. It will tell you ad nauseam about the things you need to do but not how to do them. As Charles Dickens says in his masterpiece *Bleak House*:

> "The one great principle of English law is to generate business for itself."

And this, to a large extent is true of many professions. If I tell you HOW to do it, then you won't need me and that means I can't charge you a fee. This certainly appears to have been true when *PAS 55* was produced and things have not improved with *ISO 55000*. These standards are complex and need extensive, no, I mean expensive, advisers to enable you to comply.

This book seeks an alternative approach – that of self help. It contains a set of simple-to-follow steps which should enable anyone to produce a workable asset management system without recourse to specialized consultants. It is predicated on the principle of "let's do it like this" rather than on lofty statements of requirements. After completing the basics, you should understand whether you need to get help with accreditation rather than having to rely on others from day one.

All that is required is a small basic staff, possible even just one person, though two is always better, with a remit from management to compile a working system. All of it can be done on a PC with simple software such as Microsoft Office though a database may be preferred to a series of spreadsheets. Either way, data collection should be completed in spreadsheets and, if required, it can be migrated to database software at a later stage. Keep it simple!

One key factor, is the commitment of management as all departments with physical assets are required to participate when their area of business is under consideration.

You will make mistakes along the way but they should be minimal and should not involve great expense as long as only your time is involved. Most of these procedures were based on simplified versions of the more complex ones used in the core business of Severn Trent Water but, if you only have three weeks to teach a system in a developing country, then simplicity is the key factor. Best skim through to the end before embarking on surveys as this should avoid you having to repeat steps which should be taken in the strict order herein.

The AMS has linkage to other aspects of the business especially those relating the physical assets which the company requires to carry on its business:

- Vision and Mission Statements
- Policy development and review
- Strategy development and review
- Reporting
- Grant Management
- Finance
- Capital investment programming
- Demand Forecasting
- Condition assessment
- Levels of Service
- Depreciation and Valuation
- Operation and maintenance

An AMS consists mainly of an inventory of assets - usually contained in a database - and a computerized system that aids valuation and compiles output in such a way that the priorities for investment can easily be recognized and acted upon. The figure below shows the typical layout of an AMS and the interaction of the components. Obviously operations and maintenance have a big part to play in most of the components.

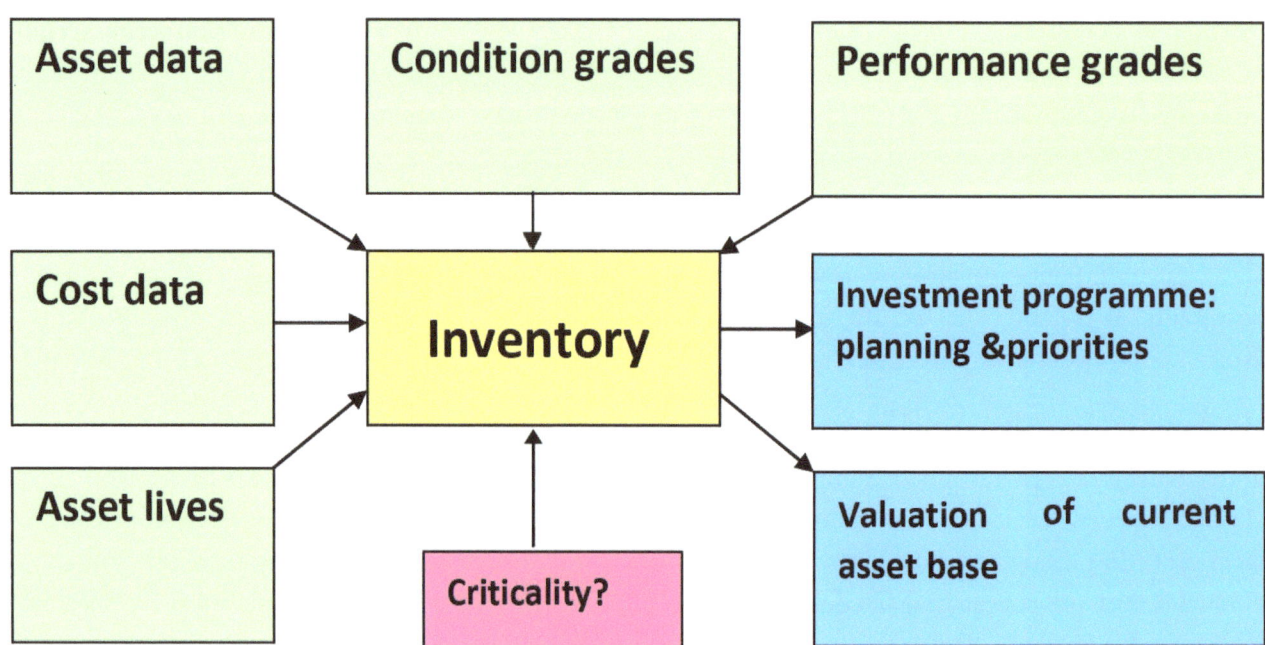

Typical AMS structure

4

As well as the internal connections there are links with other stakeholders, both internal and external:

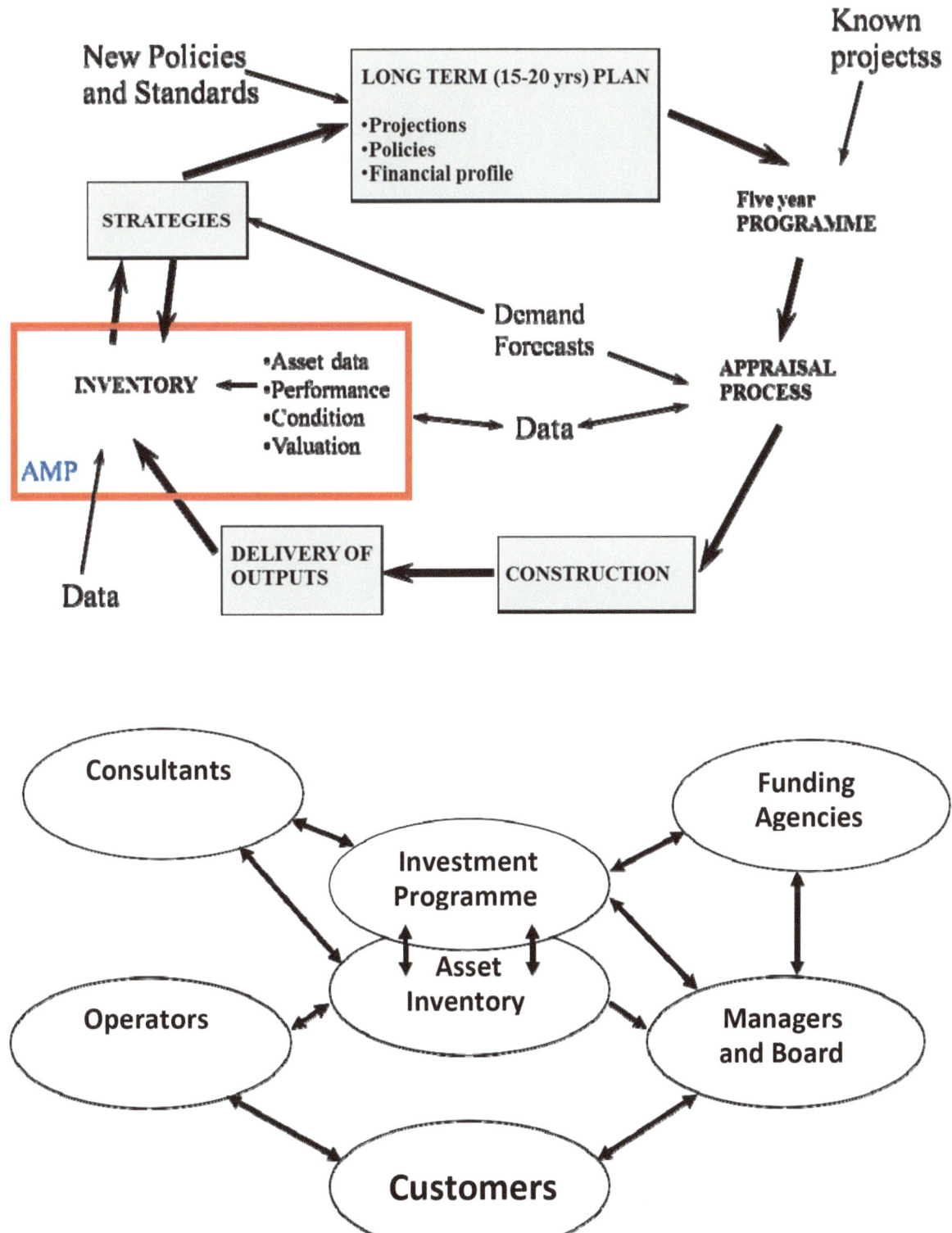

Asset Management – Two Very Different Approaches

For the sake of convenience, I will call the two systems 'Maxi' and 'Mini'. The maxi approach seeks to encompass virtually the entire functioning of a business whilst the mini approach is a low level tool enabling a company to look after its assets in the long term.

The Maxi Approach

Let's look at the definition of asset management taken from PAS 55, the early industry bible created by the Institute of Asset Management:

"systematic and coordinated activities and practices through which an organization optimally and sustainably manages its assets and asset systems, their associated performance, risks and expenditures over their life cycles for the purpose of achieving its organisational strategic plan"

There's not much wrong with this, that is if you understand it, and as long as you're a Daily Telegraph reader you should be able to. But what it results in is a grand concept which has a grave tendency to take over almost everything in its path. Here's a typical organization based on it:

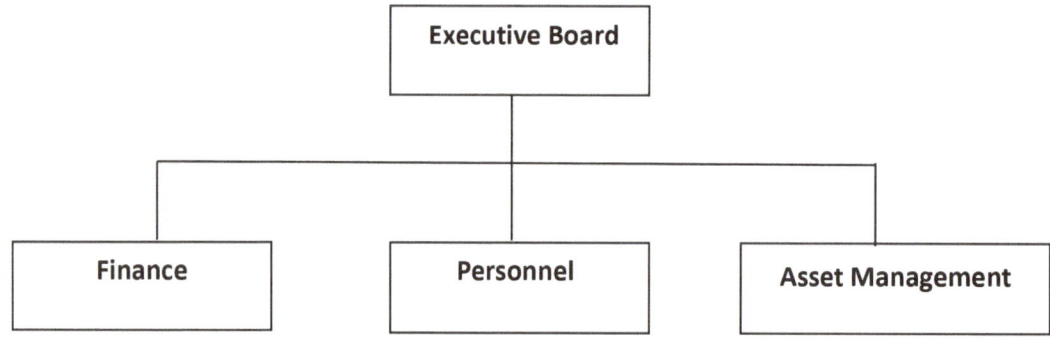

This requires that all of the functional activities of the company are situated in one department resulting in the need to create a sub tier of directors with departmental responsibilities covering operations and maintenance, investment and customer services, etc.

Policies, strategies, objectives and plans are used to drive the system so that AM becomes an integral part of virtually the whole organization. The problem here is that the object of the exercise gets lost amongst the complex management structure with its stringent requirements and drivers which tend to be simplistically target based. If placed alongside a quality management system (ISO 9000) and/or an environmental management system (ISO 14000), the company is likely to find itself spending all of its time on managing the systems and lose sight of its basic objectives. This happened in my own company and took years to sort out.

The Mini Approach

Let's look at a simpler definition of asset management based upon its original concept related to the capital maintenance of assets:

"a management tool enabling a business to plan for the replacement of its assets prior to them becoming obsolete or failing to adequately perform their functions"

This is a simple definition which is based upon a practical system of listing and categorising assets so that prioritised strategies may be drawn up enabling the organisation to ensure that its objectives and performance targets are met.

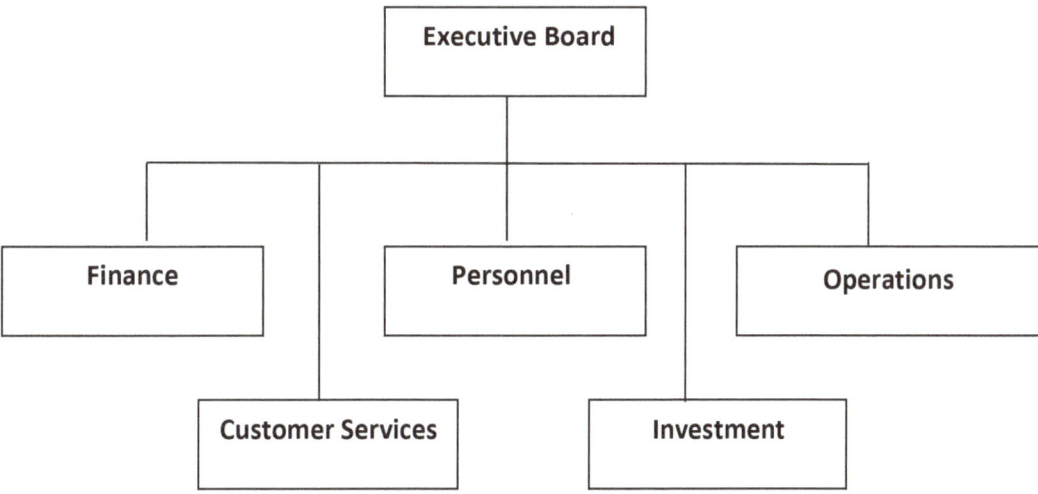

In this scenario asset management is part of the investment function sitting alongside strategic planning and programme management. Design and construction may be part of the investment function or outsourced but will come under the control of the director responsible for investment.

This fundamental structure places asset management in the context where it was always intended to be – a tool for the business to use for its capital maintenance function. There is no argument about its vital importance to the business but there is concern: that using the systems specified in PAS 55 results in it getting above its station and becoming a many headed monster. If one looks at the recent history of similar developments it is easy to see how they come and go with great regularity and with dubious outcomes. Examples include:

- Resource planning in the late 1970s
- Quality management in the 1980s
- Environmental management and risk management in the 1990s and now
- Asset management in the 21st century

Asset management is an essential part of any modern business but it needs to be kept in its place and seen in the context as was originally planned before it was hijacked.

The Inventories

The inventory is fundamental to the whole system. It contains all of the detail that is necessary to make the system work. Without a quality table of properties the AMS is worthless. The following is an example of some of the essential components of a basic inventory of the physical assets which make up a water treatment plant:

- Serial number of the data set
- Reference(s) – there may be more than one reference for an item of plant especially if the AMS is replacing an old one
- Name(s) of the plant and alternative name – again there may be more than one
- Location 1 – the name of the city/town/village
- Location 2 – usually a grid reference
- Group – any grouping that it belongs to
- The type/nature of the process on the plant
- Whether the asset is structural or consists of mechanical and electrical components (this distinction is essential as their asset lives are quite different)
- Its capacity (what it is capable of treating)
- Its throughput (what is actually going through the process)
- Its operational status – under construction; operational; not working; abandoned
- Its condition grade
- Its performance grade
- Its asset life
- The date of coimmissioning (note <u>not</u> its age!)
- The replacement cost (the MEAV)
- Remarks

When deciding on the content of the inventory it is useful to think carefully about the level of detail that is required for the purposes of asset management. Too much detail could swamp the system but too little means that it will not perform its functions.

Compiling a table at the plant level would be crude and would not enable the users to be able to distinguish between the different processes that make up the plant. Mimicking the level of detail which is required for a maintenance system means that there is too much data and the system is unwieldy.

It is clearly recommended therefore that any system designed to cover a plant should be compiled at the process level.

Compiling an inventory for any elongated collection of assets such as pipelines or cables is somewhat different but again, the level of detail is crucial. Such systems may form a grid structure or be dendritic in nature; either way the reference numbers of the individual links and nodes is crucial. The UK water industry developed a system of referencing based on the underlying Ordnance Survey maps which means that every pipeline (sewer or water main) has a unique identifier. A typical data table for sewers would look like this:

- Pipeline reference
- Upstream node
- Downstream node
- Material
- Length
- Gradient
- Function (foul; surface water; combined)
- Asset life
- Date of construction
- Condition grade
- Performance grade
- Cost of replacement (MEAV)

Some inventories contain more detail such as invert levels. Manholes (which are listed as the u/s and d/s nodes) are not usually listed separately but are included in the replacement costs. It is likely that the inventory concerning elongated assets (as distinct from point/nodal assets) will be far bigger than any of the other inventories.

Whilst based on examples of water industry assets, the examples above can be easily adapted to any other industry but need to be carefully thought through. A few trial runs are needed before the format is finalized. Examples covering highways and social housing are appended.

Land and buildings are listed in a separate table as, in particular, their valuation process is different being based on market values rather than replacement costs. In addition, land has an indefinite asset life.

- Name
- Location
- Function
- Area
- Use
- Operational status
- Owner
- Occupier
- Last valuation
- Date of valuation

Other assets, such as vehicles and mobile plant also need their own inventory as their functions are quite different:

- Registration
- Owner
- User
- Type (car; van; wagon; mobile plant; fixed plant)
- Date of purchase
- Cost
- Current value (market value)
- Condition grade
- Performance grade

Whilst the four examples above cover the commoner types of asset that are available to a business, there may be a need for more tables, for instance, a mining company could need separate tables for mineshafts and tunnels. There is no better way to determine the best way forward than to look at examples from others and extract that which is useful for yourself.

Compiling the inventory itself is best done in stages. The first stage is to look for existing tables of information. These may reside in strange places and some will contain large amounts of data especially if used for maintenance purposes. The basic tables are best constructed in a spreadsheet format rather than a database as this is user friendly and flexible. If required, the data can be migrated to a database later.

All assets should be photographed with a digital camera and the photos cross referenced with the inventory reference number. It is now common practice to store larger files, such as photographs, in the cloud.

The properties indicated in the examples above form the headings across the spreadsheet as limiting the width of the sheet aids the production of print-outs whereas the number of rows (i.e. assets) can be as great as required. Database printouts tend to look a little bald and not user friendly. If a friendlier output is desired, place the database output into a spreadsheet and prettify it to taste. A basic example of an inventory sheet, before addition of the condition and performance grades, follows:

SNo	CDM order	Fac ID	Name	W'field	Status	ROU	MWID	Depth	Operator	Elev'n	Contour Elev	Remarks
1607		300-1	Khaldyeh Well 21	13	OP	8	AL1748		Mafraq			
1608		302-1	Khaldyeh Well 30	13	OP	8	AL1037		Mafraq			
1609		301-1	Khaldyeh Well 24	13	OP	8	AL1030		Mafraq			
1610	164	012-1	Slechat Spring	73	OP	10	AB0578		Shouna N	22	15	
1611	163	013-1	Slechat Well 8	73	OP	10	AB1362	320	Shouna N	-43	-31	
1612	165	015-1	Slechat Well 3	73	OP	10	AB1369	223	Shouna N	-131	-104	
1613	112	017-1	Krayymeh Well 1	52	OP	10	AB1380	294	Shouna	-159	-159	
1614	216	104-1	Ain Al Tanour Spring	29	OP	1	AH0510		Ajloun	652	638	
1615	061	107-1	Zuqaiq WPS 1	26	OP	1	AJ0580		Ajloun	164	120	
1616	219	108-1	Ain Rason Spring	32	OP	1	AH0506		Ajloun	769	754	
1618	097	109-1	Arjan Well 1	37	NW	1	AH1000	545	Ajloun	706	665	
1619	020	111-1	Halawa Well 2	12	OP	1	AB3152	520	Ajloun	304	258	
1620	218	122-1	Ain Jana Spring	31	OP	1	AJ0582		Ajloun	860	830	
1621	215	124-1	Fowarah Spring	27	OP	1	AJ0510		Ajloun	875	862	
1622	062	127-1	Ain Al Saluce Spring	28	NW	1	AJ0524		Ajloun	955	932	
1623	063	128-1	Anjara WPS	35	NW	1	AJ0528		Ajloun	910	891	
1624	114	135-1	Krayymeh Well 2 Ain Um Qasem	52	NW	10	AB1361	188	Shouna N	-137	-140	
1625	220	136-1	Ain Um Qasem Spring	33	OP	1	AK0521		Ajloun	286	214	
1626	042	177-1	Safsafa Well 2	21	OP	1	AK1016	589	Ajloun	734	705	
1627	174	008-4	Tabagat Fahel Well 3	76	OP	10	AG3004	10	HQ		-51	

Referencing

All databases will require a serial number as the basis for any data set. Whilst a spreadsheet will function without one it is best to assign one as the first data field in any sheet.

It is up to any business to design its own system of referencing which is appropriate to its undertaking, however, it is always wise to consider some aspects of a well designed system. The key to this is to get the length right – not too short and not too long whilst imparting as much information as possible. What follows is a system used in several undertakings which we referred to as 'PoP references' meaning Plant or Pipeline references:

BOL/WTP/01/1

This is a plant reference and the first three digits refer to the location i.e. BOLsover

The second three digits refer to the type of plant, in this case a water treatment plant

The following number refers to the process on that plant in the order that water passes through it. The last number allows for sub-division of the process or for differentiation of individual items of plant as would be required for the maintenance system (CMMS). This may be adapted to cover land and buildings as well as vehicles

SP1354/1234-SP1354/1238

This is a pipeline reference designating the nodes at either end of the pipeline. It is based on the specification in the WRc report STC25.

SP1354 is the number of the relevant OS sheet.

In the case of a sewer, the first number (SP1354/1234) is the upstream node (manhole) and the second one, the downstream node. For potable water the direction of flow is not relevant.

Computerized analysis systems for sewers and water mains use a completely different system of numbering which is not necessarily relevant for AM purposes but may be included as an additional field.

Unlike the procedures for grading, the development of a customized system will not affect the working of the AMS.

Condition Grading

The process of grading assets according to their condition can commence in parallel with the compilation of the inventory. Meeting with operators to explain the process of AM affords the opportunity to start data gathering. Operators whilst taking pride in their best assets, will often take the opportunity to go into detail about those items of plant which are in need of excessive maintenance and hence replacement.

A grading team will normally consist of two persons – one from the AM team and an operator. This is essential to maintain consistency. Whilst the opinion and input of the operators is essential, the AM team must provide balance to avoid subjective assessment.

Grading is primarily based on what the asset looks like, not its performance (that comes later). In the case of certain assets, such as pumps and motors, this may require knowledge of what it looks like when stripped down rather than just the external appearance. Operators are normally aware of this.

Each asset is assessed according to the five standard grades <u>which should never be amended</u>. Whilst standard descriptions are used, it is normal for these to be backed up with sample photographs. This was a process pioneered by the UK, Water Research Centre when looking at the internal condition of gravity sewers using CCTV. The five grade system has become a standard in most industries and countries where AM is used. Those that change it do so at their peril as they lose consistency with others including back-up.

1	Excellent
2	Good
3	Adequate
4	Poor
5	Awful

Examples of 'adaptation' include substituting 'average' for 'adequate', 'very good' for 'excellent' and 'very bad' for 'awful'. This is often due to users thinking that they do not have sufficient assets in a particular grade to warrant it and so seek to change it. If this is the case then any change should not be made to the basic table but to the detailed descriptions which are appended to the basic statements. An example of typical condition definitions follows:

Typical Condition Grades

CG	Grade	Asset Description
1	Excellent	• in 'as new' condition • electrically safe • requires only routine maintenance
2	Good	• shows only superficial signs of wear and tear, protective coatings still intact, no corrosion • electrically safe • infrequent minor failures
3	Adequate	• all components functioning well • significant signs of wear and tear, minor corrosion • electrically safe • regular minor failures but no major failures
4	Poor	• still functioning but requires substantial maintenance to be kept going • electrically safe but marginal • regular minor failures and occasional major failures
5	Awful	• frequent (monthly) breakdowns, not working or abandoned • electrically unsafe

The grading of pipelines, especially buried ones is more difficult as observing the interior of a pipe is problematical especially if it is pressurized. CCTV surveys are now common and it is normal to grade groups of pipelines of a similar age with the same condition grade. This may not be strictly accurate but it does approximate to the actual condition as the grouping will tend to include only pipelines which were constructed from the same material and at the same time i.e. under a single contract. This is especially true for those which serve housing and industrial estates. Pipelines under main roads were often constructed as part of a major pipeline and at the same time.

BRIDGNORTH – JUNE 1984
Before Lining

BRIDGNORTH – JUNE 1984
After Lining

The generic grading table for pipelines issued by OFWAT follows:

Condition Grade	Definition	Action
1	No failures, fully complies with modern standard	None required
2	No significant failures, not quite consistent with modern standard (less than 1 failure/km / annum)	Non required
3	Deterioration beginning to be reflected in service levels or increased operating costs (less than 3 failures /km/annum)	Investigate
4	Considerable corrosion affected service performance, nearing end of useful life, frequent bursts (3 to 5 failures/ km/annum)	Plan for asset replacement in short term
5	Substantially derelict and source of service problems, no residual life (more than 5 failures/km/annum)	Immediate asset renewal required

It may be argued that this is a mixture of condition and performance grades but, if bursts are an indication of condition, then it may be accepted as valid. An alternative set of definitions based on the percentage area of a pipe's cross section could be developed for both sewers and water mains.

Condition Grade	Definition
1	100% cross sectional area; surface/lining intact
2	100% cross sectional area; minor surface abrasions
3	99% cross sectional area; minor corrosion
4	95% cross sectional area; significant corrosion
5	less than 90% cross section; major corrosion problems

The illustration above shows what can be done by rehabilitating an existing grade 5 pipeline and bringing it up to grade 2 thus prolonging its life for another 50 years.

Examples of assets in grade 1 ('excellent')

Examples of assets in grade 2 ('good')

Examples of assets in grade 3 ('adequate')

Examples of assets in grade 4 ('poor')

23

Examples of assets in grade 5 ('awful')

Levels of Service and Performance Grading

The assignment of performance grades (PGs) is the most complex and demanding stage of the whole process in setting up an AMS. This is usually because the underlying 'levels of service' criteria have not been developed and agreed upon. Unlike 'condition', which relies on what the asset looks like, 'performance' relates to how well it does what it is designed to do. In setting out the criteria for performance levels many system developers fall into a simple trap – they set the criteria using physical measurements based on design criteria.

An example would be where the PG for a flood bank is related to the design level of the bank. It should actually be related to the level of protection against flooding given to those who benefit from it. Thus it would be based on the frequency of flooding of a property rather than a level. A further example would be where the PG is related to the quantity of water produced by a plant measured against its design capacity. It should relate to the service provided to the customer, not what the plant designer thought at the time it was built.

Never forget the customers!

The 'levels of service' (LoS) compiled within the AMS should be based on the service that the company has undertaken to provide to its customers. Where a department has only internal customers, i.e. other departments, then they are treated as 'customers'.

The definitions will vary according to local aspirations, thus a water company, in a developed country, would define 'adequate' as always implying a 24/7 supply of water but in a developing country, this might be seven hours per day for seven days a week.

Each LoS criteria is measured against five set levels which must be debated and tested before final adoption. These are intended to allow the full range of services to be described without undue detail. They are always based on the following subjective descriptions:

1. Excellent
2. Good
3. Adequate
4. Poor
5. Awful

No attempt should be made to change this basic structure as simplification makes it too crude and complication gives too many grades to be worthwhile. Any customisation should be at the detailed stage when the definitions are attached to the grades.

When setting out the basic grades the 'excellent' level 1 definition will be that of the aspiration for the service, i.e. the service that is desires to provide. The awful' grade should describe the lowest standard currently supplied to a significant proportion (say 3-5%) of customers. The 'adequate' grade will be about half way between these but is subject to comparison with the results obtained from any customer survey. It should reflect an 'adequate' level of service. In practice a certain amount of debate is required to get the grades to settle down. If there is no consensus then a definition will be about right if there are as many arguing for it to go up as there are arguing for it to go down.

Examples of detailed grades, based on water supply in a developing country could be based on those that follow:

Continuity of Supply

For a water company this service level is crucial to the whole exercise and will depend on the way the system is operated as it will, to a great extent, reflect the imposition of 'scheduling' on areas of supply according to the availability of water. It is therefore the first and most important one to measure. Hours per day, days per month and many other methods may be used but hours per week is the simplest and most objective:

CS1	Continuous Supply
CS2	Supply > 120 hours per week
CS3	Supply > 84 hours per week
CS4	Supply >48 hours per week
CS5	Supply < 48 hours per week

It can be argued that the lower level (CS5) should be 'no water' and that tankered supplies should be included.

Water Quality

Water Quality has three distinct aspects to it relating to bacterial, toxicological and 'customer perception' (aesthetic issues). Only that for the first is appended below:

BQ1	Compliance with National Standard based on WHO*
BQ2	No more than 1 failure per year
BQ3	No more than 3 failures per year
BQ4	No more than 12 failures per year
BQ5	Always needs boiling to make potable

*World Health Organization standards are now promoted as a guideline for the development of local standards

Interruptions in Supply

IS1	No more than 1 per year
IS2	No more than 5 per year
IS3	No more than 10 per year
IS4	No more than 20 per year
IS5	More than 20 per year

An 'interruption' requires definition which could be: "an unplanned (i.e. not scheduled) interruption in supply due to pipeline or plant failure lasting 8 hours or more".

Pressure and Flow

PS1	Better than 20m at normal time of day
PS2	Between 15 and 20m
PS3	Between 10 and 15m
PS4	Between 5 and 10m
PS5	Less than 5m at normal time of day

'Normal time of day' would exclude the two peak hours and probably the eight hours overnight.

FL1	More than 25 lpm
FL2	Between 15 and 25 lpm
FL3	Between 10 and 15 lpm
FL4	Between 5 and 10 lpm
FL5	Less than 5 lpm

This is measured at the first tap in the premises, again at normal time of day.

Sewage Treatment

Most sewage treatment plants will have a formal discharge standard against which to measure compliance.

DQ1	Compliance with consent (95%ile)
DQ2	75% compliance but no discernible pollution
DQ3	50% compliance but no discernible pollution
DQ4	25% compliance and occasional pollution
DQ5	Non-compliance or discernible pollution

Asset Lives

The accountants' approach to asset replacement is:

- produce a listing of all assets and their acquisition costs
- assign each asset with a life in years
- depreciate each asset cost using a depreciation curve (usually a 'straight line')
- add new assets acquired during the year at cost
- sum the asset values to give a new total

This has the advantage of simplicity but does not deal properly with condition and performance or deal with assets which have been improved during their nominal lifetimes. Some assets will fail before the end of their expected life whilst many others last longer. The AMP approach uses the condition and performance of an asset, combined with its nominal life, to prioritise the timing of its replacement and to calculate its current worth. It is useful in producing draft priority listings and for the planning of long term investment needs.

The tables below provide a suggested list of asset lives for use in an asset management system. It is provided for guidance only, as an aid to those who are in the early stages of setting up an AMS. The definitions may be adapted to local conditions (for instance in aggressive climates) where appropriate.

Airports

Asset type	Typical life	Range
Runway surface	25 years	20 – 40 years
Runway base	60 years	50 – 70 years
Taxiway surface	30 years	20 – 40 years
Taxiway base	60 years	50 – 70 years
Terminal building	50 years	40 – 80 years
Baggage handling	20 years	10 – 30 years
Refuelling systems	15 years	10 – 20 years

Buildings and Land

Asset type	Typical life	Range
Freehold land	Indefinite	N/A
Leasehold land	Remainder of lease	N/A
Historic buildings	Assess individually	100 – 500 years
Brick and concrete structures	60 years	50 – 80 years
Steel and cladding structures	25 years	20 – 50 years
Wood/temporary buildings	10 years	5 – 40 years
Brick/concrete/stone walls	80 years	60 – 100 years
Palisade fencing	30 years	20 – 40 years
Other boundary fencing	15 years	10 – 20 years

Electronics

Asset type	Typical life	Range
Mainframe computers	10 years	3 – 15 years
Networks	5 years	3 – 10 years
PCs	3 years	2 – 6 years
Embedded electronics	10 years	5 – 15 years
Traffic lights	25 years	15 – 40 years

Highways and footpaths

Asset type	Typical life	Range
Carriageway formation	100 years	50 – 150 years
Kerbs and channel	60 years	20 – 100 years
Asphalt surfacing	25 years	20 – 40 years
Bitumen surfacing	20 years	15 – 25 years
Tarspray surfacing	10 years	8 – 12 years
Flagged footpath	20 years	15 – 25 years
Bitumen footpath	15 years	10 – 20 years
Brick paved footpath	30 years	20 – 50 years
Gravel footpaths	12 years	10 – 15 years

Highway ancillaries

Asset type	Typical life	Range
Bridge structure	80 years	50 – 100 years
Bridge joints	15 years	10 – 25 years
Concrete footbridge	50 years	40 – 80 years
Steel footbridge	40 years	25 – 50 years
Retaining wall	100 years	50 – 100 years
Safety barriers	20 years	10 – 30 years
Bus shelters	20 years	10 – 30 years
Boundary fencing	20 years	10 – 50 years
Street lighting	25 years	20 – 50 years
Culverts	See water below	

Parks

Asset type	Typical life	Range
Grassed areas	indefinite	
Wooded areas	indefinite	
Planted areas	50 years	arbitrary
Play area equipment	15 years	10 – 20 years
Catering facilities	See buildings	
Roads and footpaths	See highways	
Gates and boundaries	See land and buildings	

Housing

Asset type	Typical life	Range
Structure	60 years	60 years
Roof	60 years	60 years
Chimney	60 years	60 years
Doors and windows	25 years	25 years
Plaster and decoration	10 years	10 years
Kitchen	20 years	20 years
Bathroom	20 years	20 years
Electrics	25 years	25 years
Heating	20 years	20 years
Plumbing	30 years	30 years
Communications	10 years	10 years
Garden	50 years	50 years

Vehicles and Plant

Asset type	Typical life	Range
Small vans and cars	3 years	2 – 5 years
Heavy vehicles	10 years	7 – 20 years
Mobile plant	15 years	10 – 20 years
Specialized vehicles	20 years	10 – 30 years
Fixed mechanical plant	15 years	10 – 20 years
Fixed electrical plant	12 years	10 – 20 years
Lifts	20 years	10 – 30 years

Water

Asset type	Typical life	Range
Impounding dams	60 years	50 – 100 years
Treatments plants	50 years	40 – 60 years
Service reservoirs	50 years	40 – 60 years
Pumping stations	50 years	40 – 60 years
Wells	30 years	10 – 50 years
Steel pipelines	30 ears	10 – 50 years
Plastic pipelines	60 years	50 – 100 years
Cast/ductile iron pipelines	80 years	60 – 100 years
Concrete/clay pipelines	80 years	60 – 100 years
System valves	10 years	5 – 20 years
Bulk meters	10 years	5 – 20 years
Service meters	5 years	2 – 15 years

Note the substantive difference in lifetimes between structural assets (typically 50+ years) and those of a mechanical nature (typically 10-15 years). The short lifetime of computers is largely due to technical advances rather than them wearing out.

Valuation

Whilst performance grading is the most difficult part of the overall process, valuation is probably the most complicated. Accountancy rules get round this problem by simplifying the process to a great degree as indicated in the last chapter (on asset lives). But their purpose is to simply have a means of writing assets off in the accounts so that they do not distort the charges in any individual year by swamping it with capital spending. This works well for that purpose but does not give a meaningful assessment of the current value of the assets which the company owns. To do this, both condition and performance need to be factored in along with the replacement rather than the original installation cost.

The next task in compiling the inventory is to add in an estimate of the capital cost of replacing the asset. This is not based on a straight, like-for-like replacement but what would you replace the asset with, if things had moved on and there better ways of doing it? Thus we have the concept of MEAV – the Modern Equivalent Asset Value. This is the capital cost of an asset which could replace the existing one but using the best thing available now – rather than when the original asset was purchased.

The MEAV needs to be calculated for each of the processes or pipelines that we have added to the inventories. This can be done in two ways:

- a 'bottom-up' approach which does a detailed calculation of the cost of components and their installation in a completed form; this is the way that quantity surveyors build up the cost of assets
- a 'top-down' approach which takes the whole cost of a plant or group of links, and then breaks it up into percentages which are then applied to the whole

The first method tends to result in a gross under-estimate of the assets' costs but the second is usually quite reliable for plant. When assigning costs to assets, it is beneficial to use a stable currency rather than the local one which may be subject to inflation. Thus, I have always used the USD when valuing.

In a developed economy, which has a strong manufacturing base, structural costs will tend to make up two thirds of the overall cost and mechanical/electrical, one third. In countries which have to import mechanical/electrical equipment, the ratio tends to be reversed.

The best method, overall, of computing MEAVs for plant, is to take the historical costs of past projects and list them according to the size of the plant or grouping and then pro-rata the gross, inflated cost to arrive at costs for new plant. Pipelines tend to be costed using the bottom-up method but with due attention to the overheads and add-ons which are frequently neglected.

Having all of the necessary data included in the inventory, a current valuation can be calculated. Almost all companies use different techniques to calculate the current value of the plant and linear assets but the following methodology is based on sound, common-sense principles. It can be adapted according to the wishes of the company.

Firstly we need to calculate the remaining asset life (RAL). This is based on the condition and performance grades as a percentage as shown in the table below which has the PG in the left-hand column and the CG along the top:

Condition Grade

Performance Grade	1	2	3	4	5
1	100	87	75	62	50
2	87	75	62	50	37
3	75	62	50	37	25
4	62	50	37	25	12
5	50	37	25	12	1

Thus, if both CG and PG are excellent (grade 1), the asset will reflect 100% of its replacement cost (the MEAV). If both grades are 5, then it will reflect only scrap value. An asset with 'adequate' for both grades would have an RAL of 50%. '0' is not used as it can create problems in some of the downstream computations. This is a 'regular' table which has the percentages evenly spaced.

The RAL is now multiplied by the MEAV to give the current asset value (CAV). If all of the CAVs are summed, then this is the estimated current value of the company's assets. A worked example follows:

A small company has a single plant with three processes; two pipelines; one building and one vehicle. Using the regular table they can be valued as:

Process one, AL 20 years, MEAV $1,000, is CG2 and PG3; RAL is 0.62 so 0.62x1,000 = $620;

remaining life = 12.4 years

Process two, AL 15 years, MEAV $ 3,000 is CG3 and PG3; RAL is 0.50 so 0.50x3,000 = $1,500;

remaining life = 7.5 years

Process three, AL 10 years, MEAV $2,300 is CG4 and PG4; RAL is 0.25 so 0.25x2,300 = $575;

remaining life = 2.5 years

Pipeline one, AL 50 years, MEAV $4,300 is CG3 and PG3; RAL is 0.50 so 0.50x4,300 = $2,150;

remaining life = 25 years

Pipeline two AL 60 years, MEAV $6,000 is CG3 and PG3; RAL is 0.50 so 0.50x6,000 - $3,000;

remaining life = 60 years

The building ($25,000) and the vehicle ($3,000) are at market values thus have a value of $28,000

Total value of company assets = $35,845

Obviously process three would be the priority for replacement but in the meantime it would warrant extra maintenance to keep it working.

Some argue that a badly performing asset (often one which is the wrong type, for instance) would still have a considerable value as it could be sold. In this case, the table can be skewed to take this into account. Obviously it would not apply to buried pipelines so some common sense is need in deciding which approach to take. A sample skewed table is shown below:

Condition Grade

Performance Grade	1	2	3	4	5
1	100	75	50	25	10
2	85	65	40	20	7
3	70	50	30	15	4
4	60	40	20	10	2
5	50	30	10	5	1

Outputs from the AMS are best handled manually as the algorithms required for automatic output are complex. As regards the output for the CIP, this will tend to concentrate on assets in the grade 4 and grade 5.

Investment Planning and Project Appraisal

Introduction

Investment Planning (or capital investment programming) is an essential task carried out, albeit often intuitively, by most organisations. Only with a system for obtaining new assets and the extension and replacement of existing ones, when they become obsolete, beyond repair or overloaded, can companies and utilities ensure the effectiveness and efficiency of their business.

UK systems are largely driven by the requirements of the Regulators and are based on an underlying assumption of service levels that do not exist world-wide. Many computerized management systems also possess a level of sophistication that is neither needed nor affordable in developing countries. Thus the term 'appropriate technology' is paramount in determining what is achievable and desirable. Even moderately sophisticated systems will fail if they need constant outside support to maintain them. Of equal importance is the expense of computers and software. PC based systems with proprietary software, that can be purchased locally, are infinitely more likely to succeed than bespoke systems running on expensive hardware. Keep it simple.

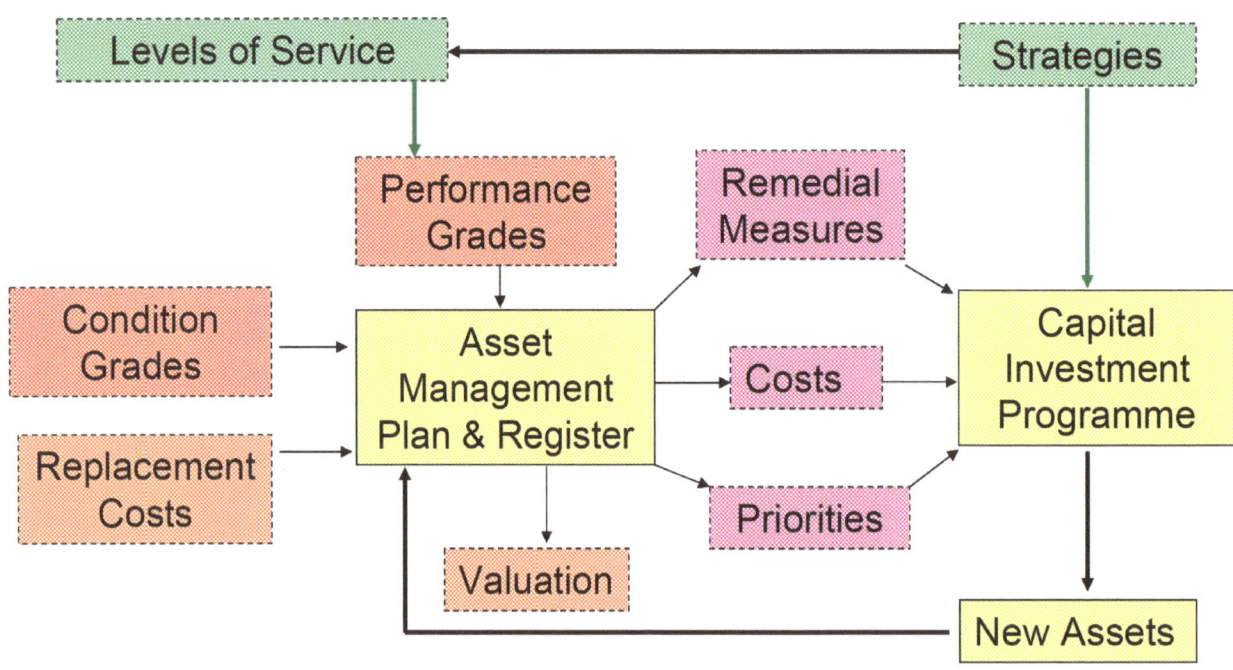

There are four essential components concerned with the overall management of capital assets:

- Asset Management Planning
- Strategies
- Programme Management
- Project Appraisal

This chapter provides an organised approach to setting up a comprehensive system for investment planning and control, adapted to the needs of developing countries though not all of the components are necessary for an effective system. It is based on experience of the successful, and cost effective, implementation of such systems internationally.

The Big Picture

The biggest problem, as with any cyclic activity (Fig 1 The Asset Management cycle), is knowing where to start. Without any external force requiring a system to be set up, many managers see an investment management system as usurping their traditional role in deciding what to build, resulting in a loss of control and their status in the organisation. Nothing could be further from the truth. The issues that result in loss of control are usually political in nature resulting from a breakdown in the provision of services and the exertion of influence to provide or restore services to particular groups of customers, often based on political considerations. A properly formulated and well managed system has its own in-built defences against unwarranted interference and results in the best use of resources to the benefit of the whole community.

Initial implementation is often the result of project requirements set out by funding agencies who are unwilling to contribute resources until the situation can be objectively assessed and they can be assured that the funds will be applied in a controlled way to meet the needs of the community. Typically the first step is the compilation of an asset inventory and valuation of the assets. This often runs in parallel with short term emergency improvements in maintenance standards applied to key items of plant.

Programme Management

Programme management is frequently viewed as an unnecessary task or an infringement in senior management's role. Whilst the function involves essential, communication skills and clerical tasks, it is immensely important in controlling the progress of schemes, the achievement of outputs and the cash flow to support the schemes. In carrying out this function he will normally monitor each project in a progression of stages:

1. Feasibility and appraisal
2. Detailed design
3. Construction
4. Commissioning and handover
5. Post appraisal

A computer programme is essential to keep this information up-to-date and in a useable form. In the first instance a simple spreadsheet may be used and this can be developed into a database as the need arises. A dedicated PC is normally adequate for this work.

The programme is first developed by listing existing schemes and is gradually refined over a period with the information and system becoming gradually more objective. The Programme Manager is central to this activity and holds a crucial post in the organisation. He is responsible for the management of the programme and all of the data contained in it. He is, however, a service provider rather than an implementer and his main skill is in keeping everything running smoothly. His main objective is to avoid surprises and eliminate costly mistakes. The procedure which follows is based on tried and tested practices and can adapted to almost any environment. It consists of a series of stages which eventually result in the construction/installation of new or replacement assets.

Form A : Identification of Need (IoN)

This preliminary form is used to register a problem which requires capital investment. It includes:

- A description of the existing service or asset problem
- The location e.g. operational plant name, geographic area, distribution zone etc.
- A general indication of benefits i.e. how many customers will receive improved service or product quality

It could look like this:

FORM A Identification of Need

Project reference			
Title			
Cost	$	Delivery Date	
Location			
Beneficiaries			
Drivers			
Short description			

Additional fields can be added such as 'Service' can be added if required but this is intended to be a simple form just notifying the Programme Manager of the need for the scheme. Whilst information is kept to a minimum at this stage, it is essential to include the need for investment based on a failure in service level.

Form B : Identification of Options

The next stage in the programme is to identify the options which could be developed to solve the problem(s). This avoids the temptation for operators to settle on their preferred solution without consideration of alternatives. The essential options to be identified concern the different approaches involving a one-off capital cost versus high annual maintenance/operating costs. It could be based on this:

Project reference			
Title			
Cost	$	**Delivery Date**	
Location			
Beneficiaries			
Options	Option 1: keep existing plant		
	Option 2: renovate existing plant		
	Option 3: replace plant with new one of same type		
	Option 4: replace plant with new type		

Form C : Appraisal and Recommended Option

This is the main stage of project appraisal and would provide the outcome of the appraisal using the one most relevant to the business (in this case DCF). It summarises the outcome of the calculations and goes on to recommend which option should proceed to the detailed design stage. Appraisal involves the use of a number of tools to assist managers and politicians in their investment decisions. These tools involve a mixture of disciplines but are predominantly financial which may be run using standard packages on a computer:

- **Discounted cash flow**

Usually involves analysis of total capital and revenue costs over a period (TOTEX) for assessing options which are aimed at producing similar outcomes:

- **Cost benefit analysis**

Used to compare alternative approaches involving different costs but producing a range of potential benefits.

- **Return on capital employed**

Used by business to assess the annual rate of return on the capital used, usually to provide a new asset.

- **Profit and Loss**

Used by business to determine whether or not to invest in a new asset.

- **Break-even**

Used to determine when an asset will start to pay for itself if it generates an income.

The latter three are normally only used to assess assets purchased for business purposes as they rely on an income for comparison. In a service utility these financial considerations are often over-ridden by statutory requirements.

Beside the financial assessments described above, appraisal must confirm the benefits are achievable and that the estimated costs are reasonable. Timescales are also subject to scrutiny. Fundamental to most water projects is demand forecasting which establishes the existing and projected water usage figures upon which the proposals are based. Other modern techniques include:

- Environmental Impact Analysis
- Sustainability Analysis
- Life Cycle Analysis
- Risk Analysis

The latter issue looks at the likelihood and effects of failure. Appraisal may be undertaken by specialists or by the project promoters but in the latter case must be subject to scrutiny by the Client. The form could be based on this:

FORM C Recommended Option

Project reference			
Title			
Cost	$	**Delivery Date**	
Location			
Beneficiaries			
Option costs over 20 years (TOTEX)	Option 1: $20,000 Option 2: $23,500 Option 3: $28.000 Option 4: $18,500		
Preferred option	Option 4: replace the existing plant with the new type of plant as this would be the lowest overall cost over a period of 20 year operation.		

The form should be accompanied by a report which explains the project in some detail. It will explain the problem(s) giving details of the location of the assets and those customers who suffer an inadequate level of service. Issues like the pollution of watercourses are included. The report should be supported with plans showing the location of the assets and potential beneficiaries and a summary of the detailed calculations which were carried out to determine the preferred option.

In the case of smaller schemes, Forms B and C may be amalgamated into a single submission.

Form D : Approval to Let Contracts

Once the project has completed the design stage it goes out to contract and, at this stage costs are firmed up and timescales detailed. Instead of 'Delivery Date' a spending profile can be appended or it can be left to the Programme manager to determine.

FORM D Contract Approval

Project reference			
Title			
Cost	$100,000*	**Delivery Date**	
Location			
Beneficiaries			
Scheme	Construction contractor X: $55,000 Construction contractor Y: $65,000 Plant supplier Z: $45,000		
Recommendation	The bids of contractor X and supplier Z be accepted		

* Plus design and supervision costs

Appended: full list of tenders and monthly spending profile

Form E : Commissioning and Handover

Once the construction is complete the contractors will hand over the assets to the client based on the company's procedures which will be 'signed off' when the plant is seen to be operating satisfactorily. Final contract costs are recorded and explanations given for any significant overspend. This is the stage at which the assets are formally recorded in the inventory as operational and the contractor enters into any relevant maintenance/guarantee phase. When this expires a formal handover is made and recorded.

Project reference				
Title				
Cost	$116,807	**Delivery Date**		
Location				
Beneficiaries				
Scheme	Construction contract: $56,123 Plant contract: $45,234 Total contract costs: $101,357 Design, supervision and overheads: $15,450			
Recommendation	The assets now be recorded in the inventory as complete and operational			

The projects, following Form A submission, are all entered into the Capital Investment Programme (CIP) with costs and timescales appropriate to the stage of advancement in the programme. This will generally make up the Five-year Rolling Programme which is used by most utilities. Private companies may adopt their own formats and timescales.

In addition to the five-year programme, it is useful to consider the longer term as this can be crucial in terms of long-term capital planning. Normally a 20 or 25 year timescale is appropriate in order that peaks and troughs may be avoided. After the initial five years, which are detailed above, most of the later spending will consist of the replacement of existing assets plus provision for any known areas of growth, whether expansion or increased use of the service. The main purposes behind this programme, which is highly speculative, is to avoid peaks and troughs in the capital spend profile and hence smooth things out. It may be appropriate to design a post-appraisal form in order to learn from mistakes.

Some organizations will also compile a short term programme in order to keep tabs on current spending. This will tend to cover the previous year and the two following years on a monthly basis. An example of a ten year programme follows:

Project	Prev	2003	2004	2005	2006	2007	2008	2009	2010	2011	2012	Total
Division 1												
Anna Regina				1,250,000	1,250,000							2,500,000
Wakenaam Island							370,000	370,000				740,000
Div 1 Strategy									2,700,000	2,700,000		5,400,000
Division 1 sub total	0	0	0	1,250,000	1,250,000	0	370,000	370,000	2,700,000	2,700,000	0	8,640,000
Division 2												
Barrica	344,000	1,592,466										1,936,466
Leguan Island	115,000							730,000	730,000			1,575,000
Poudn/F'ship strat	6,700,000											6,700,000
Poudn/F'ship storage							1,500,000					1,500,000
Parika				1,250,000	1,250,000							
Division 2 Phase 2									2,000,000	3,000,000	500,000	5,500,000
Division 2 sub total	7,159,000	1,592,466	0	1,250,000	1,250,000	0	1,500,000	730,000	2,730,000	3,000,000	500,000	19,711,466
Division 3 EBD												
Eccles/Friendship	505,000	3,900,000										4,405,000
Elevated Storage							300,000					300,000
Uppr East Bank Strat							900,000	600,000				1,500,000
Division 3 EBD sub total	505,000	3,900,000	0	0	0	0	1,200,000	600,000	0	0	0	6,205,000

A typical Ten year investment programme

Strategic Planning

A 'strategy' is a plan of action for the conduct of a (military) campaign. Thus it will include statements on objectives, the existing situation, deficiencies, resources and the available technical tools to do the job. Whilst this is widely accepted in the field of military endeavours, and the subject of extensive training, it has not always been the case in the development of water services where each project tends to be of an ad hoc nature. The number of strategic plans which a business needs to consider can be listed:

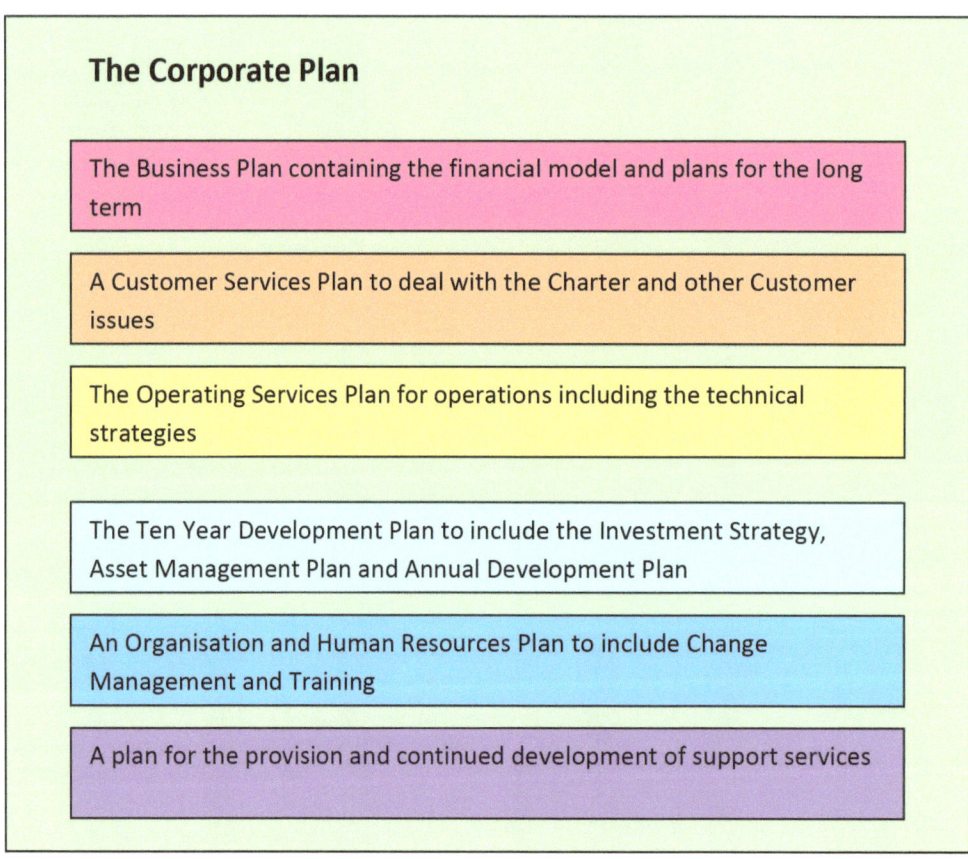

The Corporate Plan

The Business Plan containing the financial model and plans for the long term

A Customer Services Plan to deal with the Charter and other Customer issues

The Operating Services Plan for operations including the technical strategies

The Ten Year Development Plan to include the Investment Strategy, Asset Management Plan and Annual Development Plan

An Organisation and Human Resources Plan to include Change Management and Training

A plan for the provision and continued development of support services

The Asset Management Plan (AMP) is very much concerned with the replacement of individual assets whilst Strategic Planning is more likely to be concerned with upgrading sets of existing assets, proposed extensions to systems or completely new developments.

The methods by which strategies are carried out are crucial to success in the long term. Generally the 'master plan' approach involving a ten year cycle of investigation and implementation is too inflexible to provide sustainable solutions compared with the continuous system with in-house management and adaptable control.

Investment strategies can be process or area based. They can be used to introduce, for instance, new potable water standards across a whole country or they could be used to optimise the operation of a distribution system including mains, reservoirs and boosters. Thus the objective could assess all of the sewerage problems in an area (the Drainage Area Study approach), or they might involve the upgrading of all of the booster pumps in a distribution system. In some cases they may be a mixture of the two. Leakage reduction and mains rehabilitation strategies are common.

Based on the existing asset and grading data, additional surveys are undertaken to confirm the nature and extent of problems. Objectives are compiled based on proposed levels of service. Thus the difference between the existing and desired scenarios can be seen. From these considerations analysis of the plants and/or pipelines will provide notional solutions which can be priced and carried forward for appraisal and inclusion in the investment Programme. The process can be summarized as follows:

- Set an objective to be achieved in tandem with a target date for achievement
- List the existing assets and survey them for condition
- Undertake performance grading on the existing assets
- Carry out a gap analysis
- Identify what is required to close the gap and meet the proposed service levels within the life of the assets
- Compile a list of projects with cost estimates and timescales and submit them to the investment programme

The ten year sewer strategy, which was delivered on-time and on-budget, split the cities and major towns of the region into discrete 'drainage areas'. The size of the areas, at that time, was dictated by the ability of computers to carry out the necessary hydraulic analysis of the draining system in the area. The Cities were split up to analyse each area and to find out, using CCTV, where structural decay was present. Following the hydraulic (performance) and structural (condition) assessment, a prioritized list of projects was drawn up which became the basis of the CIP. A similar strategy, although somewhat lagging in timescale, drew up a programme of rehabilitation schemes for the distribution networks.

All businesses and utilities should consider which of its business practices require a strategic analysis in order to bring about a continued service to its customers without undue interruption to that service. Only with satisfactory service can a business maintain its customer base and hence its income stream.

Criticality

Criticality and risk management are linked in several ways and almost all businesses incorporate them into their processes either formally of informally. Criticality is the identification of critical assets whilst risk management is concerned with the measures that are needed to mitigate the effects of failure. There is more on a possible system of risk management for settlements and cities in the chapter on Disaster Management.

There are numerous suggestions as to how criticality should be calculated and whilst some are quite simplistic, others can be very sophisticated involving complex equations. When developing my first asset management system, I was presented with a complex scheme developed by two water engineers who had taken over two weeks working on their system for water supply. It involved scoring for schools, hospitals, government buildings and even the President's house. I added their information to the plant inventory and then ranked the assets in order and printed out the listing. After this, I placed the assets in order of size based on the throughput (though capacity would have served as well) and printed that list out. When placed alongside eachother, there were only minor differences in the order, which leads to a simple conclusion – the bigger it is, the more critical it is – and this is borne out by common sense.

However, there are two distinct aspects to criticality – the micro and the macro. The micro approach concerns the identification of individual items of plant or pipelines which are crucial to the continued operation of the plant or system. The macro approach looks at a whole system and identifies which components are crucial. The diagram below illustrates the former approach as the borehole pump and the pump to the elevated storage are the critical components – regardless of the size of the plant. A power failure would knock both of them out.

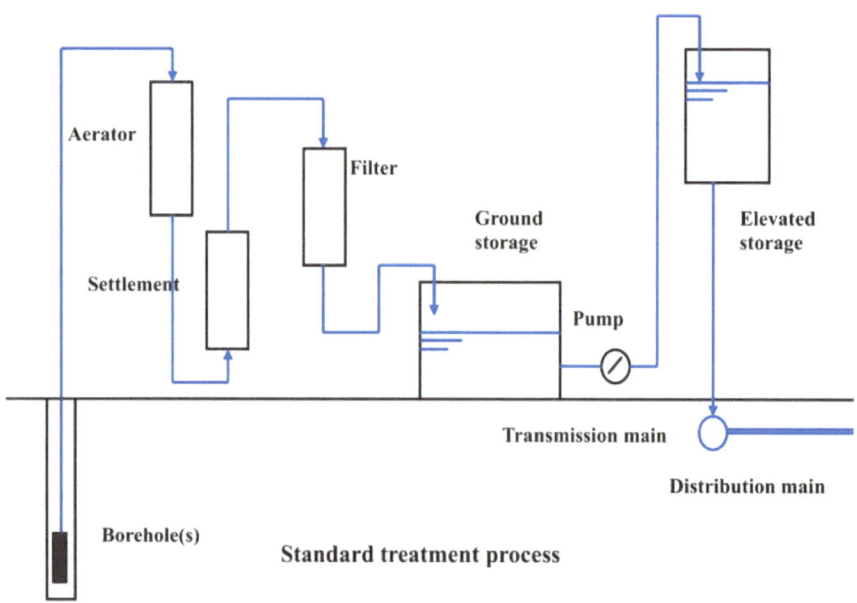

In an asset management system, criticality might be assessed and recorded as a simple numerical value for instance, using the five grade system which we are now familiar with:

1. assets of national security importance
2. assets of national importance not involving security
3. assets of local importance serving only local areas
4. assets serving areas of lesser importance
5. assets of no importance on any evaluation

These definitions are highly subjective and have not been tested to my knowledge. The key question, if you want an objective system which is not based on size alone, is where do you rank hospitals and do they rank higher than the President's house?

Most practitioners simply take account of this issue intuitively when prioritizing investment. How often have you heard the view "We must do that first because…"? In most countries investment in the capital city takes priority because government buildings are seen as critical but, in many scenarios, there is also a political element which underlies investment based on which areas voted for the party in power. Manifesto pledges can outweigh any commitment to a balanced approach.

If a more logical process is required then the procedure should require that the remaining asset life be included in some manner to give added weight to consideration of criticality. Many will prefer to simply apply a manual adjustment to the investment programme to favour the critical assets and would invest in mitigation measures which effectively reduce the probability and/or the consequences of failure. Thus, in the example above, a second borehole might be interconnected and the second pump might be duplicated to provide back-up. Where power failure is the main threat, supplies are often duplicated and, where this is not possible, a stand-by generator installed. Water distribution systems, with storage, generally have a redundant layout so that a burst pipe simply entails the isolation of the affected link whilst the burst is repaired.

With the advent of modern technology, it is now common to install real-time monitoring of all critical assets with breakdown warning and a link to a central control.

Maintenance and CMMS

Whilst the foregoing sections have dealt with the capital aspects of asset management, the regular and efficient maintenance of critical plant is paramount to the effective day-to-day operations of any business. Whilst funding agencies have frequently expended great sums on capital refurbishment and premature replacement, simple plant maintenance has often been ignored. Whole systems have failed due the lack of spares and the management necessary to see that they are effectively used.

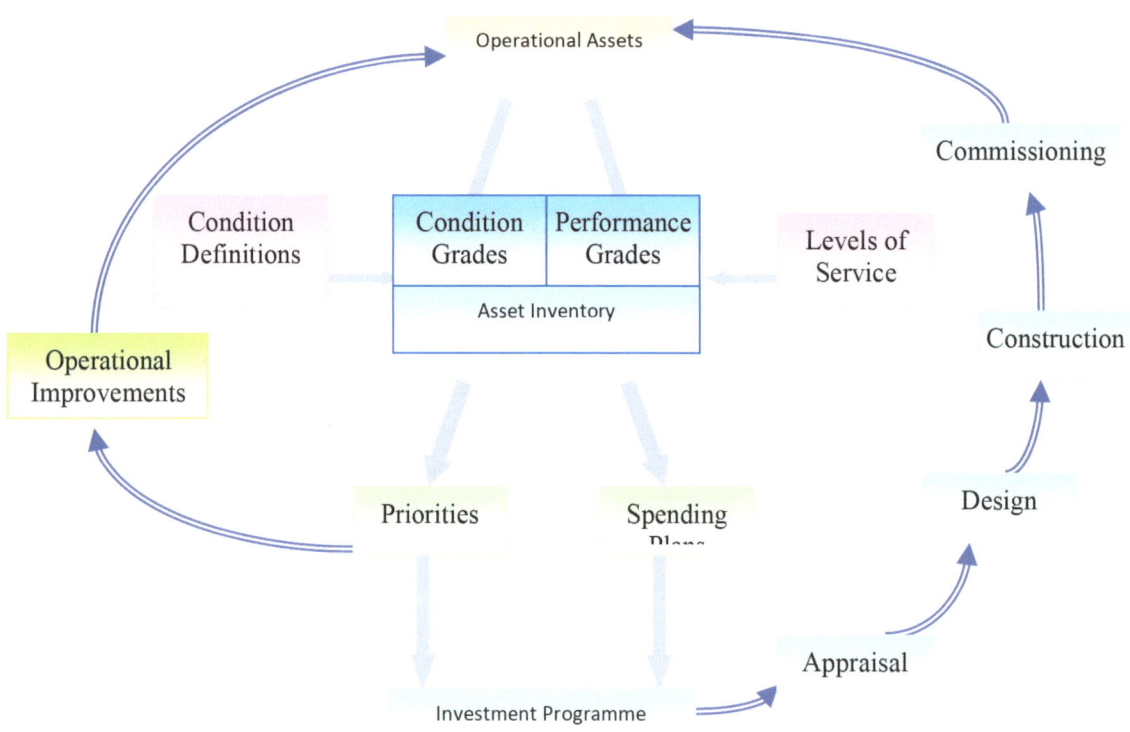

There is much common ground between capital and maintenance management though the latter tends to concentrate on rotating mechanical plant rather than pipelines. Trying to use the same management systems for both plant maintenance and asset management is fraught with difficulties and, unless properly managed, can result in a more expensive solution than keeping the two systems apart. That said, the common ground between them should be recognised and systems should use the same inventory as a base with common reference numbers wherever possible. The long term Asset Management Plan for capital investment should also be supported by Operational Plans containing levels of expenditure in maintenance and operation.

It is not my intention to write in detail about maintenance systems but to indicate how they can be simply co-ordinated with the AMS. Maintenance is generally considered to be a 'revenue' function which means that it is funded from the current year's income, whereas asset management is a 'capital' function, funded by borrowing. Other than that, there are subtle differences in the needs of their supporting systems. Often seen as the greasing of rotating mechanical plant, maintenance needs a level of detail which is an order of magnitude greater than that required for asset management. Whilst the latter generally records assets at the process level, maintenance requires each individual item of plant to be recorded. In addition, it concentrates on mechanical and electrical plant rather than structures.

There are many excellent computerized systems on the market and they contain much valuable information for the compilers of an inventory though, they will often have no interface with the AMS. At the very least they should have a common referencing system so that each of the system users can easily compare information in the two inventories. This is possible by subdividing the AM reference by a single digit. Thus pump number three in the activated sludge process at Minworth might become: MIN/ASP/PS/3. A degree of common sense is required in addition to agreement between the 'owners' of each system.

The setting up of a computerized maintenance system (CMMS) requires a similar procedure to that employed with the creation of an AMS:

- set up a detailed inventory of all plant
- identify critical items of plant
- identify plant with high failure rates
- set up schedules
- set up procedures
- implement and test
- revise and fully implement

All of this seems a little mundane but then there are many bells and whistles which can be adopted, some of which will improve the system and some will not. Amongst these is 'Reliability Centred Maintenance' or RCM which concentrates maintenance resources on those items of plant which are most likely to fail and will often consider monitoring and telemetry to warn of failure.

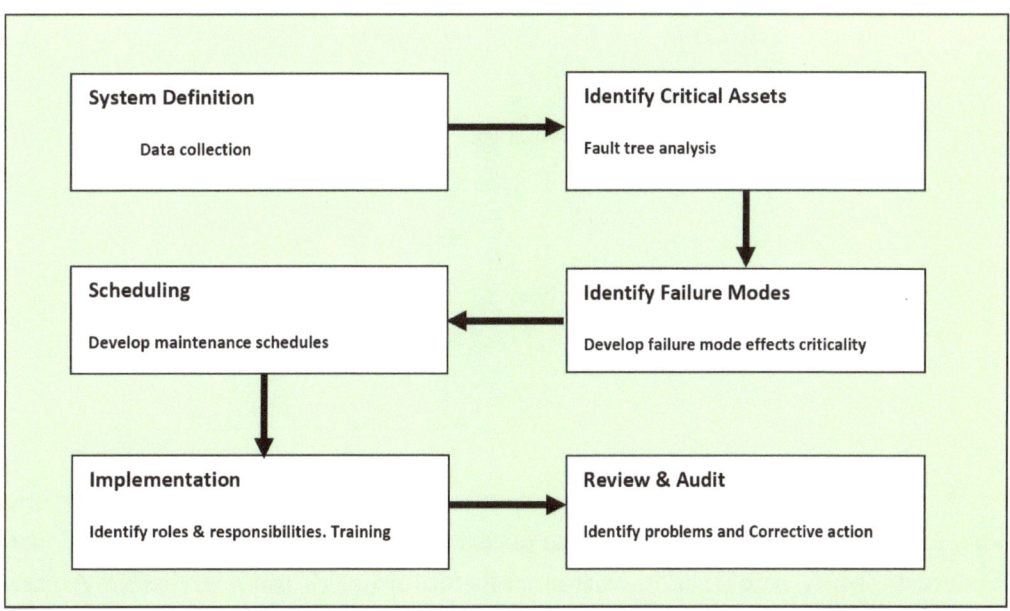

In addition to the various add-ons, management has to decide on its overall approach to maintenance which can be set out as a form of hierarchy:

- failure based systems whereby action is taken only after failure has occurred i.e. breakdown maintenance
- minimal maintenance of critical plant whereby regular maintenance is scheduled only for critical items of plant
- regular maintenance of all plant involving a system with daily/weekly/monthly schedules of tasks for all items of plant
- technology based monitoring and control – add-ons which use such things as vibration monitoring to predict the early signs of impending breakdown – then use telemetry to provide warning of failure
- predictive systems based on plant history which formalizes the instinctive knowledge of operators who generally know which items of plant will break down

Most businesses will choose a system that is somewhere in between these approaches and will have some form of computerized support system to organize and keep track of things. The maintenance of pipelines is more problematical. Normal, or day-to-day maintenance usually involves simple actions such as flushing or jetting to clear debris. Repairing bursts and collapses is only done in response to incidents. Most other maintenance, involving rehabilitation etc. would generally be considered to be of a capital nature and therefore part of the AMP and/or a strategy.

The introduction of ISO 9000 brought new ideas into maintenance and it is now common practice to produce procedures for each item of plant. This is a simple documented set of steps which tell the operator and the maintainer what to do, when to do it and in what order including health and safety issues. An example, which could be produced on a film covered A4 sheet, but is now more likely to involve a QR code, could contain steps such as those listed below:

Maintenance schedule

Plant:	Submersible pumping station maintenance

Ref:	MIN/STP/PS/P1and2	Manager:	SA

Created:	24/09/2020	Updated:	

Purpose and Scope

Steps to be taken for the weekly maintenance of submersible pump stations

Responsibility

This procedure should be carried out by a trained NVQ2 qualified fitter

Equipment

Pump gang van equipped with tools and clean water jet

Procedure (plant)

- Ascertain who else is present on site and what other procedures are likely to be carried out
- Switch off power feed to pumps and lock out; place 'locked-out' notice in place
- Open the wet well and pull up pump 1
- Examine inlet for signs of blockage and clean with water jet
- Return pump 1 to well and repeat procedure for pump 2
- Switch power back on and run both pumps while breaking up any debris in well with water jet
- Return pump operation to normal duty and standby
- Close well and lock
- Complete station log and gang log with timings

This procedure should be read in conjunction with the 'Submersible Pumping Station Safety Guide' and the Operators' procedure for this type of plant.

Disaster Planning and Asset Management

Abstract

The factors which are common to all kinds of disaster involve: the risk (what is the likelihood of an occurrence); the consequences (what happens due to an occurrence) and mitigation (what measures are appropriate to minimise the effects of an occurrence). These have not previously been combined to produce a method of comparing one location with another, independent of the type of risk or type of development. The basic concepts of asset management can be adapted to provide a framework which would enable the various factors to be combined in an organized way. Asset management and disaster planning generally use a scale one to five to quantify aspects of their severity and both utilise inventories to store information on relevant aspects. In the electronic age it is possible to collate information on a global scale but little has been brought together in a coordinated format for the benefit of practitioners in the field of disaster management. A possible way forward is suggested which could be of benefit to all stakeholders by presenting a common format which could form the basis of a global database for the collection and dissemination of information.

Introduction

The term 'disaster management' (DM) suggests that disasters can be managed. This apparently flies in the face of common sense but examination of the factors associated with DM leads to a more pragmatic view. A disaster itself is not manageable - if it were then it would most likely not be a disaster at all. What we actually mean by DM is the planning, preparation and mitigation of the effects. For many the definition includes only reactive elements i.e. the provision of resources after the event has occurred with no attention being paid to the period before the disaster occurred. Others concern themselves only with measures to avoid or mitigate the possible effects; flood control measures and tsunami warnings are obvious examples.

The first task is to identify the risk of a disaster occurring from whatever type of occurrence and then to quantify that risk by qualitative or quantitative means. Having defined the risk, attention then turns to the other main factor – the consequences. These can also be defined in qualitative and quantitative terms using a similar framework. This is the simple five point scale, which has been borrowed from asset management, using the scale from 1 (excellent) to 5 (awful) with the addition of a zero grade.

Multiplying these two factors (risk and consequences) would give a numerical indicator in the range of 0 to 25. This, in itself, would be useful in comparing one location with another, however it is possible to take the thinking a stage further by looking at what measures might be appropriate to bring the potential disaster into acceptable limits. Using a scale of 1 to 25 enables unity to be used as a measure of comparison.

The Constituents of Disaster Management

Usually the public's perception of a disaster is based on footage in the news and waiting to see what measures will be put into effect to ease the plight of the survivors. Following this, some superficial discussion takes place about the lack of planning and the reasons for the events which have taken place. The ensuing coverage concentrates on the provision of aid by local and international agencies. Only after this immediate phase is over does a rational examination of the whole scenario take place. Thus disaster management tends to mean handling the aftermath and disaster planning means the setting up of support mechanisms for the victims. We argue here, that more emphasis needs to be placed on the time prior to the occurrence of a disaster in order to mitigate the effects. Let's consider an example. In 1985, a large earthquake hit Mexico City and many people died – most due to the collapse of the building in which they lived or worked. Post planning has resulted in all new buildings in the city being able to withstand such quakes and existing buildings have been retrofitted with measures to enable them to withstand quakes. The city has since 1985, suffered a number of similar events (albeit lesser in magnitude) with very little damage and virtually no casualties. This would appear to be good planning but the risk was well known before 1985 and no substantial actions were taken. The current approach – of planning in advance for protection – makes for a more robust situation than simply planning to deal with the aftermath.

The first aspect to be considered in DM is planning and preparation and the first task is that of gathering data. Only with a sound data set can planning be undertaken objectively – otherwise it tends to be based on hearsay and anecdotal evidence. The first element of planning is to identify areas which are at risk and to equate this with the type of risk which is evident in that area, whether from natural or manmade factors.

Having ascertained what is the nature and the severity of the risk the data can be used to undertake a range of investigations before recommending what should be done to protect the potential victims. These are mainly considerations relevant to the locality but there are aspects which cut across the whole subject and this is the main area of current consideration - what should be done to avoid or reduce the full impact of a severe event? The case referred above provides a clear example whereby advance planning would have largely mitigated the effects.

In summary we have three main components to consider which are best posed as questions:

- what is the nature of the threat and the risk of its occurrence?
- what are the potential consequences?
- what are the measures which could be put into place that would mitigate damage and casualties?

In the sections below we go on to examine each of these components in more detail and them to propose an expression which would enable them to be viewed in context and compared with other similar and even dissimilar scenarios.

Risk

There is already much information available in the public domain about the potential risks which could affect localities. In order to place the following discussions into context, let us first examine these risks which fall into five (potentially overlapping) categories:

Natural disasters (earth):

- earthquake
- landslip
- subsidence
- famine

Natural disasters (air):

- storm
- hurricane/cyclone
- tornado

Natural disasters (fire):

- firestorm
- volcanic eruption

Natural disasters (water):

- flash flood
- gradual flood
- drought
- tsunami

Man related disasters

- urban fire
- terrorism
- explosion
- utility failure
- chemical/radiation

I have not considered pestilence as it does not directly affect physical assets. It would appear, however, to be the most far reaching of all disaster scenarios and Hollywood is only too keen to remind us of it.

Moving on to the severity of risk, it is proposed to classify it on the basis of the likely frequency of occurrence which can be done objectively or subjectively:

Category of risk	Frequency	Quantification
0	never	never
1	very low	1 in 1000 years
2	acceptable	1 in 300 years
3	moderate	1 in 100 years
4	high	1 in 30 years
5	extremely high	1 in 10 years or less

These are numbers and descriptions which would require assessment against a large sample of events in order to arrive at a balanced representation.

Consequences

Obviously there is an issue about the potential effects of an extreme event or 'consequences'. There is little point in expending resources to protect areas where no-one lives and the heavily populated conurbations require a high level of protection. This is normally assessed on an economic basis involving the cost of human tragedy (loss of life) and material losses.

A simple table is again proposed based on the six grade system:

Category	Description	Population	Predicted deaths	Typical economic damage USD
0	Unpopulated	100 or less	<1	insignificant
1	Village	1,000	1	10,000
2	Small town	10,000,	10	100,000
3	Large town/city	100,000	100	1,000,000
4	City	1,000,000	1,000	10,000,000
5	Conurbation	10,000,000	10,000	100,000,000

The main difficulty is in placing a cost on human life to incorporate it into the economic equations of cost/ benefit/. There is a great reluctance to address this issue as the value placed on a life varies considerably between one locality and another and it is considered callous to value the life of a child in a rural village as being worth less than that of a wealthy city dweller. However it must be recognised that we do this every day and the cost can be related to that which is expended, on average, on health care to prolong that life.

Mitigation

The question that now arises is: what measures should be provided to avoid or mitigate the effects of a severe event? Usually this is decided based on guesswork, intuition, economical analysis but most often political pressure. Those with the loudest voice get the most costly solutions. Whilst a comparative methodology (such as proposed here) will not give detailed answers, it should provide objective guidance on the level of protection based on comparison with other solutions across the world.

The types of mitigation measure range from simple post-incident situation management to expensive structures built to protect vulnerable environments. These might include:

- emergency services
- warning systems including telemetry
- fire breaks
- protection zones
- cyclone shelters
- earthquake resistant structures
- sea walls
- flood protection measures

The choice of a particular structure or measure is risk dependent and already well documented elsewhere but there appears to be no overall guidance to reflect the general level of protection which should be appropriate. This is proposed in the table below:

Range	Type of measures	Expenditure USD/capita
0	None	0
1-5	Off-line back up only	1
6-10	Minor structural work, off-line back-up	10
11-15	Intermediate works and standby backup	100
16-20	Major structural work and full time backup	1,000
21-25	Expansive redundant structures plus full time emergency backup	10,000

Conclusion

These factors can be combined in a simple expression:

risk x consequences / mitigation should be less than or = to 1

where the value of each of the three components is taken from the tables above.

This gives an indication of the preparedness and ability to respond to severe events in a particular location but only as a comparison with other places which have been similarly ranked in a consistent manner. The methodology would, therefore, be of limited use in individual circumstances; only after a significant database is in existence would the state of preparedness be evident especially when compared with like situations.

After development and data gathering it should be possible to test the principle and make a judgement of its usefulness. However, it is argued that the data acquisition process itself will more than pay for itself in making the information available to all those engaged in disaster management.

Appendix 1

an AMS for Water

Introduction

Asset management is an essential task carried out, albeit often intuitively, by most organisations and usually as part of the company's Investment Planning. Only with a system for the extension and replacement of assets, when they become obsolete, beyond repair, or overloaded can companies or utilities ensure the efficiency and effectiveness of their business. The practices and procedures herein have been developed from those applied in the UK water industry to ensure compliance with the requirements of the regulator.

Compilation of the Inventory

The inventory is fundamental to the whole system. It contains all of the detail that is necessary to make the system work. Without a quality table of properties the AMS is worthless. The following is an example of some of the essential components of a basic inventory which is based on a water treatment plant:

- Reference(s) – there may be more than one reference for an item of plant especially if the AMS is replacing an old one
- Name(s) of the plant and alternative name – again there may be more than one
- Location 1 – the name of the city/town/village
- Location 2 – usually a grid reference
- Group – any grouping that it belongs to
- The type/nature of the process on the plant
- Whether the asset is structural or consists of mechanical and electrical components (this distinction is essential as their asset lives are quite different)
- Its capacity (what it is capable of treating)
- Its throughput (what is actually going through the process)
- Its operational status – under construction; operational; not working; abandoned
- Its condition grade
- Its performance grade
- Its asset life
- The date of construction (note NOT its age!)
- The replacement cost (the MEAV)
- Remarks

When deciding on the content of the inventory it is useful to think carefully about the level of detail that is required for the purposes of asset management. Too much detail could swamp the system but too little means that it not perform its functions.

Compiling a table at the plant level would be crude and would not enable the users to be able to distinguish between the different process that make up the plant. Mimicking the level of detail which is required for a maintenance system means that there is too much data and the system is unwieldy.

It is clearly recommended therefore that any system designed to cover a plant should be compiled at the process level.

Compiling an inventory for any elongated collection of assets such as pipelines or cables is somewhat different but again, the level of detail is crucial. Such systems may form a grid structure or be dendritic in nature; either way the reference numbers of the individual links and nodes is crucial. The UK water industry developed a system of referencing based on the underlying Ordnance Survey maps which means that every pipeline (sewers and water mains) has a unique identifier. A typical data table for sewers would look like this:

- Pipeline reference
- Upstream node
- Downstream node
- Material
- Length
- Gradient
- Function (foul; surface water; combined)
- Asset life
- Date of construction
- Condition grade
- Performance grade
- Cost of replacement (MEAV)

Some inventories contain more detail such as invert levels. Manholes (which are listed as the u/s and d/s nodes) are not usually listed separately but are included in the replacement costs. It is likely that the inventory concerning lateral assets (as distinct from point/nodal assets) will be far greater than any of the others.

Referencing

The referencing of water assets is crucial to the effective and efficient working of the AMS as it enables users to access data quickly, ensuring that there is no ambiguity about which assets are being interrogated.

The system of 'PoP References' is recommended. This means Plant or Pipeline reference and is based on the systems in common use in the UK. If a local or national system exists then it should be used though both can co-exist in concert with eachother so long as there is a clear understanding of their functionality.

Condition Grading

The process of grading assets according to their condition can commence in parallel with the compilation of the inventory. Meeting with operators to explain the process of AM gives one the opportunity to start data gathering. Operators whilst taking pride in their best assets, will often take the opportunity to go into detail about those items of plant which are in need of replacement.

A grading team will normally consist of two persons – one from the AM team and an operator. This is essential to maintain consistency. Whilst the opinion and input of the operators is essential, the AM team must provide balance to avoid subjective assessment.

Grading is primarily based on what the asset looks like, not its performance (that comes later). Each asset is assessed according to the five standard grades <u>which should never be amended</u>. Whilst standard descriptions are used, it is normal for these to be backed up with sample photographs. This was a process pioneered by the UK, Water Research Centre when looking at the internal condition of gravity sewers using CCTV. The five grade system has become a standard in most industries and countries where AM is used. Those that change it do so at their peril as lose consistency with others including back-up.

1	Excellent
2	Good
3	Adequate
4	Poor
5	Awful

Examples of 'adaptation' include substituting 'average' for 'adequate', 'very good' for 'excellent' and 'very bad' for 'awful'. This is often due to them thinking that they do not have sufficient assets in a particular grade to warrant it and so they seek to change it. If this is the case then any change should not be made to the basic table but to the detailed descriptions which are appended to the basic statements. An example of typical condition definitions follows:

Typical Condition Grades

CG	Grade	Asset Description
1	Excellent	• in „as new "condition • electrically safe • requires only routine maintenance
2	Good	• shows only superficial signs of wear and tear, protective coatings still intact, no corrosion • electrically safe • infrequent minor failures
3	Adequate	• all components functioning well • significant signs of wear and tear, minor corrosion • electrically safe • regular minor failures but no major failures
4	Poor	• still functioning but requires substantial maintenance to be kept going • electrically safe but marginal • regular minor failures and occasional major failures
5	Awful	• frequent (monthly) breakdowns, not working or abandoned • electrically unsafe

Levels of Service

Why do we need Levels of Service (LoS)? Many organisations operate satisfactorily without strictly defined LoS and it is possible to subjectively arrive at the right answers. However, an organised system, with defined Levels, provides a firm basis for investment decisions allowing operators to have their say in the replacement of plant. They also provide a first line defence against undue political interference and a positive basis for the attracting funding from aid agencies. The advantages can be listed:

- Reflects what the customer is getting
- Measures services and improvements
- Provides a basis for business planning
- Can be used for project planning and financing
- Allows projects to be prioritised
- Can also form a basis for operational maintenance
- Links Operations and Investment through Performance Grades

This latter issue is the fundamental difference between Asset Management and simplistic financial systems.

In any water supply area the key issue is the continuity of the potable water supplied irrespective of other factors. 'Scheduling' – the organisation of regular but intermittent supplies is the norm in many developing countries and only when the continuity of supply is considered reasonable will the other issues come to the fore. The most important of these will be potable water quality followed by pressure.

If the implementing organisation wishes to adopt a customer service approach then a 'customer needs' survey should be undertaken to determine what standards are being achieved but, just as important, what standards are desired and what is the customer prepared to pay for them.

UK systems assume that a 24 hour service will be provided but this is not universally the case elsewhere in the world where intermittent services are the norm. There is, thus, an argument for tackling the criteria in a structured manner and giving more weight to those of greater priority in the customers' eyes. Generally sewerage and nuisance aspects are seen as a lower priority but only if water resources are not affected by effluent discharges.

Thus the structure for implementation will tend to resolve itself like this:

Water Supply LoS Criteria:

- Continuity of supply
- Water Quality
- Pressure and Flow
- Resource Availability and leakage
- Interruptions to Supply

Sewerage and Environmental LoS

- Foul Flooding
- Sewer Restrictions
- Effluent Quality
- Environmental Nuisance factors

We have not concerned ourselves here with administrative and support activities which include:

- Response to letters
- New connections
- Billing complaints
- Answering telephones
- Keeping appointments
- Public information

Framework

Each LoS criteria is measured against the five set levels which must be debated and tested before final adoption. These are intended to allow the full range of services to be described without undue detail.

No attempt should be made to change the basic structure as simplification makes it too crude and complication gives too many grades to be worthwhile. Any customisation should be at the detailed definition stage when the definitions are attached to the grades.

When setting out the basic grades the 'excellent' level 1 definition can be that of the desired aspiration for the service. The 'Awful' grade should describe the lowest standard currently supplied to a significant proportion (say 3-5%) of customers.

The 'Adequate' grade will be about half way between these but is subject to comparison with the results obtained from any customer survey. In practice a certain amount of debate is required to get the grades to settle down. If there is no consensus then a definition will be about right if there are as many arguing for it to go up as there are arguing for it to go down.

Continuity of supply

This service level is crucial to the whole exercise and will depend on the way the system is operated as it will, to a great extent, reflect the imposition of water supply 'scheduling' on areas of supply according to the availability of water. It is therefore the first and most important one to measure.

Measurement, in the first instance, may be the operators' view of the supply but this should be replaced with actual measurement or observation when available. Hours per day, days per month and many other methods may be used but experience shows hours per week to be the simplest and most objective:

CS1	Continuous Supply
CS2	Supply > 120 hours per week
CS3	Supply > 84 hours per week
CS4	Supply >48 hours per week
CS5	Supply < 48 hours per week

Levels of Service for Continuity of Supply (CS)

It can be argued that the lower level (5) should be 'no water' and that tankered supplies should be included. This is one area where sub-division of the grades might be considered as an exception to the general rule of sticking with just five grades.

Water Quality

Water Quality has three distinct aspects to it and these have their own sub priorities attached. Initially WQ may address only the key issue of **Bacteriological Quality** as this causes immediate problems. **Toxicological Quality** may be incorporated later followed by **Customer Perception** which is related to the aesthetic aspects of potable water.

BQ1	Compliance with National Standard based on WHO*
BQ2	No more than 1 failure per year
BQ3	No more than 3 failures per year
BQ4	No more than 12 failures per year
BQ5	Always needs boiling to make potable

Levels of Service for Bacteriological Quality (BQ)

*WHO is promoted as a guideline for the development of local standards

TQ1	Compliance with National Standard based on WHO*
TQ2	Failure against NS for < 1 week per year BNDTSTH*
TQ3	Failure against NS for < 1 month per year BNDTSTH*
TQ4	Continuous or regular failure against NS, BNDTSTH*
TQ5	Continuous risk including short term health

Levels of Service for Toxicological Quality (TQ)

*The term BNDTSTH (but not dangerous to short term health) is suggested as a means of distinguishing between immediate risks (e.g. poisoning) and long term effects. Again 'short term' needs definition and a period of one month is suggested as a reasonable division between short and long term.

CP1	No problems
CP2	Problems up to 1 week per year
CP3	Problems for up to 1 month per year
CP4	Continuous problem with one symptom or recurring problems with more than one
CP5	Continuous problems with more than one symptom

Levels of Service for Customer Perception (CP)

The 'problems' involved in Customer Perception are ones which arrive via the potable water supplied. Other types of problem are dealt with under Environmental Nuisance. Customer Perception problems would include:

- Discolouration
- Evidence of Animals
- Unusual or severe smell
- Unusual or unpleasant taste

Interruptions in Supply

IS1	No more than 1 per year
IS2	No more than 5 per year
IS3	No more than 10 per year
IS4	No more than 20 per year
IS5	More than 20 per year

Levels of Service for Interruptions in Supply (IS)

An 'interruption' requires definition which could be: "an unplanned (i.e. not scheduled) interruption in supply due to pipeline or plant failure lasting 8 hours or more". It is clear, therefore, that this criteria will not be very meaningful until the continuity issue is resolved.

Resource and Treatment Availability

RA1	Meets demand 10 years out of 10
RA2	Meets demand 9 years out of 10
RA3	Meets demand 8 years out of 10
RA4	Meets demand 5 years out of 10
RA5	Meets demand less than 5 years out of 10

Levels of Service for Resource and Treatment Availability (RA)

'Demand' is difficult to define and probably needs a period of observation after initially setting the criteria. Treatment capacity must be included as a raw resource is not likely to be usable as a potable supply. "The peak hourly demand on the system in the dry season" is suggested as a definition for 'demand'.

Pressure

PS1	Better than 20m at normal time of day
PS2	Between 15 and 20m
PS3	Between 10 and 15m
PS4	Between 5 and 10m
PS5	Less than 5m at normal time of day

Levels of Service for Pressure of Supply (PS)

'Normal time of day' would exclude the two peak hours and probably the eight hours overnight.

Flow

FL1	More than 25 lpm
FL2	Between 15 and 25 lpm
FL3	Between 10 and 15 lpm
FL4	Between 5 and 10 lpm
FL5	Less than 5 lpm

Levels of Service for Flow at first tap (FL)

This is measured at the first tap in the premises, again at normal time of day.

Sewerage

DQ1	Compliance with consent (95%ile)
DQ2	75% compliance but no discernible pollution
DQ3	50% compliance but no discernible pollution
DQ4	25% compliance and occasional pollution
DQ5	Non-compliance or discernible pollution

Levels of Service for Effluent Discharge Quality (DQ)

'Discernible pollution' needs definition - "Pollution evident in the water to the naked eye or causing evident effects to the plant life alongside the watercourse"

Foul Flooding

SF1	No risk of flooding of property, gardens or roads from sewers
SF2	Property: 1 in 20 years Garden/road: 1 in 1 year
SF3	Property: 2 in 20 years Garden/road 2 per year
SF4	Property 5 in 20 years Garden/road 3 per year
SF5	Property 10 in 20 years Garden/road 5 per year

Levels of Service for Foul Flooding from Sewers (SF)

Blockages

SR1	Less than 1 restriction per year
SR2	Only 1 restriction per year
SR3	More than 2 restrictions per year
SR4	More than 5 restrictions per year
SR5	More than 10 restrictions per year

Levels of Service for Sewer Restrictions (SF)

'Restrictions' are generally blockages but could also be due to inadequate capacity.

Environmental Nuisance

EN1	No Nuisance
EN2	Occasional Nuisance but not to cause discomfort
EN3	Noticeable nuisance for up to 1 month per year
EN4	Noticeable nuisance for up to 3 months per year
EN5	Regular, continuous or gross nuisance or risk to health and safety

Levels of Service for Environmental Nuisance (EN)

Nuisance from environmental factors arising from activities of the business/utility would include: flies, litter, noise, vermin, dust, traffic or other environmental disturbances to cause discomfort to the average person.

Asset Lives

The appended table (APPENDIX 1)of suggested asset lives is included to enable those of a conservative disposition to include it within the asset inventory against each item of plant and pipeline. This enables ready comparison to be made with the accounting asset valuation and can be useful in determining profiles of financial requirements for the replacement of assets.

Asset lives can be used in the following processes:

- Depreciation within the accounts
- Traditional method of Evaluating of the business
- Long term investment planning
- As a guide to capital replacement

Assets can be subdivided into types, each with their own lives; the main categories are:

- Land and buildings
- Engineered constructions
- Pipelines
- Mechanical & Electrical plant
- Electronics
- Vehicles and mobile plant

These grades are suggestions - if you don't like them, convene a representative panel and debate them until concensus is reached.

Appendix 2

an AMS for Highways

Introduction

There is a noticeable lack of consistency involving AM practices which have become commonplace in other industries. Research into the literature for AM in the highways sector reveals that there are systems and guidance notes and some organised methodology, however, the linkage between condition assessment and levels of service is rarely made. Assessment of a widely-praised AMS for highways, developed by a reputable red-brick university in the UK, turned out to be nothing more than a condition based assessment with advice on carriageway maintenance.

This paper is about adapting the basic principles of AM, as developed by the water industry in England and Wales, so that they may be easily adopted by any government body which is responsible for the management of highways leading to a prioritized investment programme as part of an asset management strategy.

There are many ways in which AM may be implemented and consistency is notably lacking in most areas. Some businesses see it as a driver covering the replacement or refurbishment of assets nearing the end of their useful life. Others see it as an all-encompassing management system covering most aspects of the business. The merits of these contrasting approaches are discussed in:

http://felixschrodinger.wordpress.com/2010/11/13/asset-management-%E2%80%93-two-very-different-approaches/

Whichever is to be adopted is a matter for the directors.

How Asset Management Works

This is best illustrated in diagrams which show the interrelationship of the components centred on the asset inventory:

http://felixschrodinger.wordpress.com/2011/08/08/asset-management-presentation/

Slides 6 and 7 show the high level relationship of AM with other components of the management system and slide 29 shows a detailed view of how the inputs and outputs of the asset management system are centred on the inventory.

The inventory is normally a spreadsheet or simple database which includes all of the information relating to the assets to be included. The choice between databases and spreadsheets is a matter for the developer of the AMS but there are some things to consider. Spreadsheets are much easier to use especially during the data collection phase however they are not as good at selecting and sorting classes of asset for further consideration. In a database all records are locked as far as their data are concerned; if the order of the records is changed then all of the associated data will move with each relevant record automatically. This is not necessarily so for a spreadsheet and an unwary user can easily break the link between an asset and its associated data by moving things around in a table.

In the case of highways it is likely that separate tables will be required for differing types of asset, even though the processes will be the same. The inventory will normally consist of inputs including:

- Asset data
- Condition grades
- Performance grades based on 'levels of service'
- Asset lives
- Cost data

And will enable outputs:

- Ad hoc reports
- Prioritization for the investment program
- Current valuation

Each of these aspects will be discussed in some detail in the sections which follow.

Level of detail

Fundamental to the success of an AMS is the level of detail. We could choose to take a whole highway as a single asset but this would militate against any system of practical management. On the other hand including too much detail takes excessive effort and can create confusion through lack of clarity.

A highway must be assessed in two aspects: its sections by length (links) and features which exist at junctions (nodes). It difficult to design a single data table to suit both types of data so careful consideration must be given to how they are set up. A 'link' is a linear section of highway and a 'node' is a junction or other point along the highway where it is split into manageable sections. This concept is common to utilities which manage pipelines and cables but not so much in respect of highways management. It is likely, due to differing data needs that that they will be best managed in separate inventories.

Components of a highway (links)

First a highway must be defined in general (high level) terms and then split into manageable lengths which are based on any change in the basic properties. A change in construction or surfacing is often selected as a node, however, it is suggested that links should not exceed 1km in length and where not otherwise divided, existing route markers should be used. The following data is required in respect of each 'link' and 'node':

- Name
- Unique identifier and/or descriptor (e.g. A562 + detail)
- 'Link' or 'node'*
- Type of highway – e.g. motorway, A road, B road, unclassified, primary estate/distributor, local access/cul de sac
- Start and end points
- Construction – paved, unpaved etc
- Number of lanes
- Builder/constructor
- Capacity
- Average and peak throughput
- Speed limit
- Owner
- Maintainer

Having constructed the main headers for the data table, we now need to input the components of the highway which, for links, will comprise:

- Carriageway formation (CF)
- Carriageway base course (BC)
- Carriageway surface (CS)
- Kerbs and channels (KC)
- Surface water drainage Pipes, ancillaries, ponds etc. (SW)
- Guard rails (GR)
- Lane and edge lines plus reflectors (WL)
- Boundary fencing (BF)
- Lighting (LG)
- Footpath/cycleway base (FB)
- Footpath/cycleway surface (FS)

Each section of highway and component should have a unique identifier which should be self evident, e.g.: A607/17E/BC would be the base course of the eastbound carriageway on section 17 of the A607.

Components of a highway (nodes)

Information about nodes, which may be junctions or intermediate points along the length of the road:

- Bridges (which may be split into components)
- Retaining walls
- Embankments
- Culverts and subways

Major junctions generally come in three types:

- Roundabouts (traffic islands)
- Light controlled junctions
- Uncontrolled junctions

The information concerning these types of junction will vary but must include all of the components (kerbs, base, surface, etc.) as for the main carriageway but will reflect the manner in which the highway has been split. Reference to a map will be essential to show where the carriageway (link) ends and the junction (node) begins.

Ancillaries

It is a matter of judgement about how to include ancillaries; however, their inclusion in the main data tables can lead to over complication. It is suggested, therefore that the following be placed in a separate table:

- Warning and direction signs
- Gantries
- Bus shelters

The following information is then added for each individual asset:

- Asset status - in use or not (code: AB, NW, OP, UC)
- Condition grade (1-5)
- Performance grade (1-5)
- Year of construction/installation
- Asset life (in years)
- MEAV ($ replacement cost)
- Criticality (optional)
- Remarks

Status

Some inventories contain only assets which are in use. This is not quite right as even an abandoned asset has some value if only the residual land on which it resides. Codes are normally used: AB = abandoned; NW = not working; OP = operational/in use; UC = under construction. It is good practice to annotate anything which is not working with a comment in the 'remarks' column.

Condition Data

Condition grading is based on what you see rather than how well the asset performs. It is not dependent upon how well it does its job from the user's point of view which is the role of the performance grade. A standard set of condition grades is appended. Generalized definitions can be applied to most assets but not all. Some types of asset have their own defined condition descriptions such as road surfacing which may have a defined set of numerical grades. In this case, the specific asset grades much be converted to the standard 1-5 grading system.

Performance Grading

Performance grades will again, be set but are based on defined levels of service criteria. This can lead to some confusion with the condition grade especially where the road surface in concerned. This can be simplified if physical issues are contained under condition and non-physical things (such as congestion) are placed under performance. Some sample PGs are appended.

Constructed and Asset Life

Each type of asset is accorded an asset life which is based on that experienced by typical assets in a similar environment. A set of standard asset lives is appended. The year of construction/installation is also required as a baseline for the asset life. Age is not used as it changes every year and is not, therefore, stable.

Replacement cost

There are many variations on the definition of the replacement cost but this will tend to be the cost of construction at the time of the survey. Some businesses use the 'Modern Equivalent Asset Value' (MEAV) concept which recognises that the replacement asset may be different from that originally built. Whichever is used, the replacement cost must be the full cost including all contract and administrative overheads. This can often increase the unit rate shown in a bill of quantities by a factor of more than two. The costing MUST be in a stable currency i.e. one with an inflation rate less than 10%.

Criticality

Many systems include a measure of risk assessment, often referred to as 'criticality'. Whilst useful this may not be essential as, in general, the bigger the asset, the more critical it will be. Obviously motorways and A roads will be more critical than B roads or unclassified and this sort of crude assessment may suffice. If a more sophisticated system is required see:

http://felixschrodinger.wordpress.com/2013/11/14/criticality/

Remarks

A remarks field is essential so that any data which is not normal can be explained.

Output - RAL

The first output will be a calculation of the 'remaining asset life' (RAL). Some systems use simple percentages or even life in years based on the condition grade. This fails to recognise that performance is just as important; an undersized asset in perfect condition may require replacement because it is now under capacity. A typical 'look-up' table combining condition and performance is shown below. The RAL is calculated as the percentage RAL times the original asset life.

Condition Grade					
Performance Grade	1	2	3	4	5
1	100	87	75	62	50
2	87	75	62	50	37
3	75	62	50	37	25
4	62	50	37	25	12
5	50	37	25	12	1

Look-up Table showing the percentage remaining asset life (%RAL).

Output – Valuation

If the replacement cost (MEAV) is multiplied by the percentage remaining asset life, divided by 100 then we have the current asset value (CAV). This gives the current value of the asset but it is unlikely to include the value of the land on which it stands. This should be considered separately.

Prioritization

It remains to examine the asset, in areas or in groups, to determine which have the highest priority. This will include those with the shortest RAL and the highest criticality score. This is a task best done by human inspection and assessment based on the output from the AMS. Computers are not noted for their judgement in these matters. A set of projects, based on either area or asset type, can now be compiled and input to the capital investment program (CIP). Obviously this first attempt will not conform with the available funding profile or practical timescales. The program, which must also contain all new schemes, is then smoothed to take out peaks and troughs whilst allowing for available funding.

Condition Grades for Highways

There are a number of number of numerical grading systems available for use and these may be applied subjectively or objectively based on actual measurements. Amongst these are:

- Surface Distress Index (SDI)
- Ride Comfort Index (RCI)
- Pavement Quality Index (PQI)
- Structural Quality Index (SQI)

Whether one of these, or other, numerical system is adopted is a matter for local consideration and the degree of effort that the asset owner wishes to invest. Whilst such systems will undoubtedly provide a clear unambiguous system of grading, most highway managers will be aware intuitively of the grades and hence their priorities. It is arguable whether the RCI is a 'condition' issue or a 'performance' one. In this scenario it is restricted to condition.

Specific Condition Grade - Formation

The purpose of the formation is to provide a stable and regular support to the base course. Thus the frequency of failure and the regularity of the surface of the formation are pertinent.

Grade	Description
1 – excellent	Stable in all respects with no history of failure; no deviation greater than 20mm
2 – good	Stable in all respects with only very infrequent failure; no deviation greater than 35mm
3 – adequate	Stable in all respects with only occasional failure; no deviation greater than 50mm
4 – poor	Some areas of instability with occasional failures; no deviation greater than 100mm
5 - awful	Unstable with frequent failures; deviation frequently greater than 100mm

Many roads have no surfacing ('sealing' in some countries) and hence the formation also provides the running surface. In this case 'corrugation' and 'rutting' should be taken into account.

Specific Condition Grade - Base Course

The purpose of the base course is to smooth out imperfections in the formation and provide a stable base for the wearing course. The grade could be based on the same system used for the wearing course (below) or it could be related to the performance of the base alone.

Grade	Description
1 – excellent	Stable in all respects with no history of failure; no deviation greater than 10mm
2 – good	Stable in all respects with only very infrequent failure; no deviation greater than 15mm
3 – adequate	Stable in all respects with only occasional failure; no deviation greater than 20mm
4 – poor	Some areas of instability with frequent failures; no deviation greater than 30mm
5 - awful	Unstable with frequent failures; deviation frequently greater than 40mm

Specific Condition Grade - Wearing Course

The grade for the wearing course may be objectively based on a defined methodology or it may subjectively use generic grades. The advantage of an objective system is that it will take both severity and frequency into account in arriving at a combined score which is converted into a grade. An objective system, based on the Pavement Condition Index (PCI)* from Canada might look like this:

Severity	Extent	Value	Score
	none	0	8
Very slight	few	0.5	7
Slight	intermittent	1	6
Moderate	frequent	2	5
Severe	extensive	3	4
Very severe	throughout	4	3

*Establishment of Network Trigger Values for Pavement Management Rehabilitation (Donaldson R MacLeod, 2008)

Pavement Condition Index

Grade	Description
1 – excellent	PCI score 8 or better
2 – good	PCI score 7
3 – adequate	PCI score 6
4 – poor	PCI score 5
5 - awful	PCI score 4 or worse

If the country or locality has another available scheme then this should be used as appropriate.

Generic Condition Grades

The grades for other assets can be developed for them specifically or generic definitions can be used:

Grade	Description
1 – excellent	In 'as new' condition without minor defects
2 – good	Minor defects only apparent with finishes etc. but no major problems
3 – adequate	Significant minor problems which do not affect overall performance and only occasional major problems
4 – poor	Significant major issues on a regular basis which affect performance but do not affect safety overall
5 - awful	Significant problems which affect performance; unsafe

These grades are applicable, in general terms to most (non mechanical/electrical) assets and may be extended or replaced to deal with particular components where they already have specified condition grades. Where electrical components are present then the grades may be extended by adding a reference to electrical safety.

Performance Grades for Highways

The performance grades for all of the components of the carriageway are based on safety, speed and the capacity of the highway according to its ability to meet the needs of the users (customers). There are many ways to do this; the UK system is based on hourly capacity whereas in the US it is based on peak hourly flow. Whilst the assessments shown below may not accurately reflect either, they provide a basis for consideration whilst consideration is given to any local standards. Where a local standard does exist, this is used to define grade 3.

Capacity/congestion

Grade	Description
1 – excellent	Meets daily and peak hour flows with at least 20% spare capacity
2 – good	Meets daily and peak hour flows with at least 10% spare capacity
3 – adequate	Meets daily flows with some spare capacity but peak hour flows will suffer some delay
4 – poor	Just meets daily flow requirements but significant delays during peak hours
5 - awful	Fails to meet daily and peak hour flows leading to significant delays even outside of peak hours

Safety

Grade	Description
1 – excellent	No reportable accidents ever
2 – good	Only occasional reportable accidents and none serious
3 – adequate	Less than one serious accident in five years
4 – poor	More than one serious accident in five years
5 - awful	More than two serious accidents in five years

The problem with this grading is in defining the length under consideration; is a complete section of highway considered, just the asset length or should the incidents be apportioned per kilometre of length? The latter approach is the most objective, however, most accidents tend to occur at junctions.

Speed

Speed performance should always be related to the speed limit pertaining to the road.

Grade	Description
1 – excellent	Always able to travel at the speed limit
2 – good	Able to approach speed limit for in excess of 95% of time
3 – adequate	Able to approach speed limit for in excess of 90% of time
4 – poor	Frequent blocks and tailbacks
5 - awful	More than daily blocks and tailbacks

Other Asset Performance Grades

Consideration must now be given to the standards that the ancillary assets are required to perform. A few examples are given below.

Guard Rail Performance Grade

Obviously this must be assessed only where a guard rail is deemed to be necessary – usually bends, embankments, bridges and central reservations.

Grade	Description
1 – excellent	Will deflect a 40 ton HGV and prevent it from leaving its own carriageway; inherently safe
2 – good	Will deflect a 20 ton HGV and prevent it from leaving its own carriageway; inherently safe
3 – adequate	Will deflect 90% of the vehicles using the highway; inherently safe
4 – poor	Will only deflect 70% of the vehicles using the highway; not designed for HGVs; may have safety flaws
5 - awful	Will not deflect or retain average traffic; not designed for HGVs; may be dangerous in operation

Lighting Performance Grade

Obviously this must be assessed only where a guard rail is deemed to be necessary.

Grade	Description
1 – excellent	Exceeds standard by a comfortable margin with excellent reliability and low power consumption
2 – good	Exceeds standard marginally and inherently reliable with low power consumption
3 – adequate	Lighting meets standard for the highway/area and is basically reliable with adequate power consumption
4 – poor	Below standard lighting for the highway/area and with occasional malfunction; poor power consumption
5 - awful	No lighting in an area where there should be; excessive power consumption

It is possible to define the grades for all of the asset types based on the principles above. Should there a national or local standard this will form the basis of grade 3. Grade 1 is the best standard achieved locally with spare capacity and grade 5 is the worst standard achieved anywhere in the country. Grades 2 and 4 are interpolated.

Performance grades for traffic junctions are more difficult to define though safety and congestion will be the major factors in performance.

Asset Lives for Highways

Asset type	Typical life	Range
Carriageway formation	100 years	50 – 150 years
Kerbs and channel	60 years	20 – 100 years
Asphalt surfacing	25 years	20 – 40 years
Bitumen surfacing	20 years	15 – 25 years
Tarspray surfacing	10 years	8 – 12 years
Flagged footpath	20 years	15 – 25 years
Bitumen footpath	15 years	10 – 20 years
Brick paved footpath	30 years	20 – 50 years
Gravel footpaths	12 years	10 – 15 years

Ancillaries

Asset type	Typical life	Range
Bridge structure	80 years	50 – 100 years
Bridge joints	15 years	10 – 25 years
Concrete footbridge	50 years	40 – 80 years
Steel footbridge	40 years	25 – 50 years
Retaining wall	100 years	50 – 100 years
Safety barriers	20 years	10 – 30 years
Bus shelters	20 years	10 – 30 years
Boundary fencing	20 years	10 – 50 years
Street lighting	25 years	20 – 50 years
Culverts	60 years	50 – 100 years

Surface Water Drainage

Asset type	Typical life	Range
Pump station structure	50 years	40 – 60 years
Pump station mechanicals	15 years	10 – 20 years
Steel pipelines	30 years	10 – 50 years
Plastic pipelines	60 years	50 – 100 years
Cast/ductile iron pipelines	80 years	60 – 100 years
Concrete/clay pipelines	80 years	60 – 100 years

Appendix 3

an AMS for Social Housing

Background

Asset management (AM) was pioneered in New Zealand and Australia in the 1980s and has been adopted by a number of businesses in the UK. In particular it has featured heavily in OFWAT's regulation of the water industry in England and Wales where systems were standardized and methodologies refined. These procedures and systems have been used in many countries across the world enabling water (and other) undertakings to produce investment programs to look after their assets in the longer term.

Introduction

There is a noticeable lack of consistency in the housing industry involving these practices which have become commonplace in other industries. Research into the literature for AM in the housing sector reveals that there are systems and guidance notes and some organised methodology, however, the linkage between condition assessment and levels of service is rarely made. This paper is about adapting these principles so that they may be easily adopted by any business or local government body which is responsible for the management of a housing stock leading to a prioritized investment programme as part of an asset management strategy.

How Asset Management Works

This is best illustrated in diagrams which show the interrelationship of the components centred on the asset inventory:

http://felixschrodinger.wordpress.com/2011/08/08/asset-management-presentation/

The inventory is normally a spreadsheet or simple database which includes all of the information relating to the assets to be included. In the case of housing stock, a single table or spreadsheet may suffice but if different types of property are to be included then separate tables may be required, even though the processes will be the same. The inventory will normally consist of inputs:

- Asset data
- Condition grades
- Performance grades based on 'levels of service'

- Asset lives
- Cost data And will enable outputs:
- Ad hoc reports
- Prioritization for the investment program
- Current valuation

Each of these aspects will be discussed in some detail in the chapters which follow.

Asset Data

For a housing stock the following data is required:

- Unique identifier
- Address
- Type of property – e.g. house, bungalow, flat, maisonette, sheltered
- Sub type - e.g. detached, semi, mid/end terrace
- In the case of flats – the floor level
- Number of bedrooms
- With garage or not
- Construction – brick, concrete, wood etc
- Builder
- Occupied or not
- Condition grades
- Performance grades

Condition Data

Condition grading is based on what you see rather than how well the asset performs. It is not dependent upon how well it does its job from the occupier's point of view which is the role of the performance grade.

Structure

- Structure, roof and chimney
- Doors and windows
- Plaster and decoration
- Insulation

Amenities

- Kitchen (adequate layout/space and less than 20 years old)
- Bathroom (appropriate location and less than 30 years old)

Utilities

- Electrics
- Heating

- Plumbing
- Drainage
- Communications

Exterior

- Garden and fencing
- Garage and parking

Management

- Estate/block management

The grades are:

- Grade 1 = excellent
- Grade 2 = good
- Grade 3 = adequate
- Grade 4 = poor
- Grade 5 = awful

The grades which follow are simply examples of how they should look. If a minimum standard is defined in a regulation or adopted standard then that forms the basis for grade 3. Grade 1 is then the highest standard achieved within the sample of assets in the group. Grade 5 is the lowest standard experienced in the locality; grades 2 and 4 are interpolated.

Structure

Condition grade for the structure, roof and chimney		
Grade	Description	Definition
1	Excellent	As new
2	Good	Free from all defects, watertight with no sign of dampness
3	Adequate	Only minor defects, watertight and no sign of dampness, no infestation
4	Poor	Some significant defects, occasional leakage or dampness, slight occasional infestation
5	Awful	Significant defects, structurally unsound, leakage and/or dampness, regular serious infestation

Condition grade for the doors and windows		
Grade	Description	Definition
1	Excellent	As new, double glazed uPVC
2	Good	uPVC less than 10 years old
3	Adequate	uPVC more than 10 years old
4	Poor	Wood or uPVC with some defects
5	Awful	Unsound wood with significant defects

Condition grade for the plaster and decoration		
Grade	Description	Definition
1	Excellent	As new with tasteful decoration
2	Good	Plaster sound with reasonable standard of decoration
3	Adequate	Plaster sound with questionable decoration
4	Poor	Plaster has some defects and poor decoration
5	Awful	Unsound plaster, flaking or coming away in large areas

Condition grade for the insulation		
Grade	Description	Definition
1	Excellent	As new; exceeds full specification* comfortably; installed within last five years
2	Good	Close to full specification installed within last ten years
3	Adequate	Three out of four main insulations meet full specification
4	Poor	Only two insulations meet specification; installed over ten years ago
5	Awful	Only one or no insulation meets specification; installed over 20 years ago

*200mm loft insulation, double glazing, draught proofing, cavity wall insulation

Amenity

Condition grade for the kitchen/utility		
Grade	Description	Definition
1	Excellent	Good space and layout and less than 5 years old; includes washing machine, fridge/freezer and dish washer
2	Good	Good space and layout and less than 10 years old; includes washing machine and fridge/freezer
3	Adequate	Adequate space/layout and less than 20 years old; Includes washing machine and fridge
4	Poor	Poor space/layout and more than 20 years old; may not include appliances
5	Awful	Very poor space/layout and more than 20 years old; may not include appliances

Condition grade for the bathroom and toilet		
Grade	Description	Definition
1	Excellent	As new, bath, shower and separate toilet
2	Good	Less than 15 years old with bath or shower and toilet
3	Adequate	Less than 30 years old with bath or shower plus toilet
4	Poor	More than 30 years old with bath or shower plus toilet
5	Awful	More than 30 years old and in very poor condition

Utilities

Condition grade for the electrics		
Grade	Description	Definition
1	Excellent	As new
2	Good	Less than 15 years old with circuit breaker
3	Adequate	Less than 25 years old, with circuit breaker
4	Poor	More than 25 years old with fuses but passes tests
5	Awful	More than 25 years old and fails safety tests

Condition grade for the heating

Grade	Description	Definition
1	Excellent	As new with grade A boiler
2	Good	Less than 10 years old with grade A or B boiler; no breakdowns
3	Adequate	Less than 15 years old with grade B boiler, infrequent breakdowns
4	Poor	More than 15 years old with grade C boiler or worse; occasional breakdowns
5	Awful	More than 20 years old with significant faults and regular breakdowns

Condition grade for the plumbing

Grade	Description	Definition
1	Excellent	As new
2	Good	Less than 10 years old; free from all defects, watertight with no sign of leakage
3	Adequate	Less than 20 years old; only minor defects, watertight and no sign of leakage
4	Poor	More than 20 years old; some significant defects requiring repair, occasional leakage
5	Awful	More than 20 years old; significant defects, structurally unsound, leakage and/or dampness

Condition grade for the drainage

Grade	Description	Definition
1	Excellent	As new connections for foul and surface water to main systems
2	Good	Pipes free from defects and no blockages or flooding ever
3	Adequate	Pipes free from serious defects; occasional blockages which are easily cleared
4	Poor	Pipes have minor defects and suffer regular blockages
5	Awful	Pipes have serious defects and create regular problems with blockages and/ or flooding

Condition grade for the communications		
Grade	Description	Definition
1	Excellent	As new television, telephone and fast broadband
2	Good	Television, telephone and broadband installed less than 5 years ago
3	Adequate	Television, telephone and broadband installed less than 10 years ago
4	Poor	Only telephone and television connections; installed more than 10 years ago
5	Awful	Television and landline telephone only installed more than 20 years ago

External

Condition grade for the garden and boundary fencing		
Grade	Description	Definition
1	Excellent	Immaculate with secure fencing
2	Good	100% cultivated; weed free and mown lawns; secure fencing
3	Adequate	Tidy with mown grass and no litter or dumping; secure fencing
4	Poor	Only part tended with litter but no dumping; marginally insecure fencing
5	Awful	Untended with litter and dumping; very insecure fencing

Condition grade for the garage		
Grade	Description	Definition
1	Excellent	As new
2	Good	Free from all defects, watertight with no sign of dampness
3	Adequate	Only minor defects, watertight and no sign of dampness
4	Poor	Some significant defects, occasional leakage or dampness
5	Awful	Significant defects, structurally unsound, leakage and/or dampness

Management

Condition grade for management		
Grade	Description	Definition
1	Excellent	Experienced management team with defined roles and procedures to handle all eventualities, no budgetary constraint
2	Good	Good management with very adequate budget
3	Adequate	Average management with adequate budget
4	Poor	Poor management with budgetary constraints
5	Awful	Very poor management with severe budgetary constraints

Performance Grading

Performance grades are loosely based on the 'Decent Homes Standard' (DHS) criteria contained in 'A Decent Home – Definitions and Guidance for Implementation, June 2006 published by the Department for Communities and Local Government' (see addendum). However, whilst detailed and authoritative, the standard is lacking in some respects:

- It defines many of the standards using non-compliance (negative) criteria rather than positive compliance
- It makes no obvious distinction between 'condition' and 'performance' criteria
- It is over complex in many aspects
- It requires to be read in conjunction with other documents (covering risk management) and is not self contained
- It has the appearance of being written by solicitors rather than practitioners and is, therefore, less than helpful in many respects

It is advocated that the standard be used as a check list to ensure that all relevant criteria have been covered. Where differing (national?) standards are in force, the grading systems should be adapted using grade 3 as 'compliance'.

The ability to grade performance should be based on set 'levels of service'; these are defined using the same five grades listed above for condition but the assessment needs to be based on criteria which the occupier/ customer perceives rather than condition. The following are suggested:

- Structure
- Energy efficiency
- Amenity
- Utilities
- Access
- External
- Estate/block management

The problem here is trying to bring together the various aspects which have featured in previous publications. The suggested performance grades are based on the headings produced earlier:

- Structure
- Internal amenities
- Security (free from crime and nuisance)
- Safety (free from external risks e.g. flood, fire, storm, landslip, etc.)
- Energy efficiency
- Utilities
- Access
- Suitability for occupants
- Estate/block management

Structure

Performance grade for the Structure and internal safety		
Grade	Description	Definition
1	Excellent	Free from all Category 1* risks with no history of them ever being present
2	Good	Free from all Category 1* risks with no more than one ever being present
3	Adequate	Free from all Category 1* risks
4	Poor	Free from all but one Category 1* risk but not presenting immediate danger to occupiers
5	Awful	House contains significant Category 1* risks

Category 1 risks include: Serious dampness, excessive heat or cold, pollutants (asbestos, biocides, CO, Lead, radiation, and uncombusted gas).

Energy Efficiency

Performance grade for the energy efficiency		
Grade	Description	Definition
1	Excellent	EPC grade A
2	Good	EPC grade B
3	Adequate	EPC grade C
4	Poor	EPC grade D or E
5	Awful	EPC grade F or G

Amenity

Performance grade for the amenities		
Grade	Description	Definition
1	Excellent	As new kitchen and bathroom; all in working order
2	Good	Modern kitchen and bathroom; all in working order
3	Adequate	Modern kitchen and bathroom; with only minor defects
4	Poor	Older kitchen and bathroom; with a number of minor defects
5	Awful	Older kitchen and bathroom; with a number of serious defects

Utilities

Performance grade for utilities		
Grade	Description	Definition
1	Excellent	All utilities provide reliable continuous service
2	Good	All utilities provide reliable continuous service with only minor notified interruptions
3	Adequate	All utilities provide continuous service with occasional minor problems
4	Poor	One or more services provide regular but non-serious problems
5	Awful	One or more services provide regular serious problems

External

Performance grade for external risks*		
Grade	Description	Definition
1	Excellent	No reported incidents ever
2	Good	Only one reported minor incident in 10 years
3	Adequate	No more than three reported minor incidents in 10 years
4	Poor	Regular but minor incidents
5	Awful	Serious incident involving injury

External risks include: Flood, tsunami, storm, landslide, earthquake and fire. **'Minor' would usually relate to incidents affecting the outside of the property. ***'Serious' would include incidents which affect the inside of the property.

Performance grade for access		
Grade	Description	Definition
1	Excellent	Ground floor access at front and rear, car parking for more than one vehicle on site
2	Good	Ground floor access at front and rear, car parking for at least one vehicle on site
3	Adequate	Ground floor access at front and rear, car parking nearby
4	Poor	Ground floor access at front only, car parking problematical
5	Awful	Ground floor access at front and some distance from vehicle access; no parking provision nearby

The above grades would apply to traditional housing; different criteria might apply to flats and maisonettes.

Management

Performance grade for security – crime and nuisance		
Grade	Description	Definition
1	Excellent	No reported incidents ever
2	Good	Only one reported incident in 10 years
3	Adequate	No more than three reported incidents in 10 years
4	Poor	Regular but minor incidents
5	Awful	Regular incidents involving security interventions and/or court actions

Performance grade for suitability of property for occupants		
Grade	Description	Definition
1	Excellent	Each occupant has own bedroom plus one spare
2	Good	Each occupant has own bedroom
3	Adequate	No 'overcrowding'
4	Poor	Minor 'overcrowding'
5	Awful	Serious 'overcrowding'

'Overcrowding' is defined as ……………

Sheltered accommodation and flats will require different criteria.

Performance grade for estate or block management*		
Grade	Description	Definition
1	Excellent	Management have regular contact, no complaints
2	Good	Management have regular contact, occasional minor complaints only which are speedily dealt with
3	Adequate	Management have regular contact, regular but minor complaints only and dealt with efficiently
4	Poor	Contact irregular and regular serious complaints, dealt with sporadically
5	Awful	Management unresponsive and complaints not dealt with.

Asset Lives and Cost Data

The following simplified list of asset lives is suggested along with indicative orders of cost data based on replacement costs rather than market values:

Asset	Life	£ Cost
Structure	60 years	70,000
Roof	60 years	20,000
Chimney	60 years	10,000
Doors and windows	25 years	10,000
Plaster and decoration	10 years	4,000
Kitchen	20 years	5,000
Bathroom	20 years	5,000
Electrics	25 years	3,000
Heating	20 years	4,000
Plumbing	30 years	3,000
Garden	50 years	N/A
Communications	10 years	1,000

All of the essential data is now input to the inventory. It remains to compute the outputs from this, using methodologies incorporated into the software.

Remaining Asset Life

The remaining asset life (RAL) is calculated by the system using a look-up table which gives the percentage remaining asset life (%RAL):

Condition grade	Performance grade				
	1	2	3	4	5
1	100	87	75	63	50
2	87	75	63	50	37
3	75	63	50	37	25
4	63	50	37	25	13
5	50	37	25	13	1

The remaining asset life is calculated by multiplying the percentage remaining by the initial asset life, dividing by 100 to give the answer in years.

Valuation

Now that we have the percentage remaining asset life (%RAL), we can also use it to calculate the current asset value (CAV) if we multiply the asset replacement cost by the %RAL divided by 100 to give an answer in £. The current asset value can be used in the accounts but will differ from any calculations used by the accountants who use a 'straight line depreciation curve'. Change, on a year- by-year basis in the current value, can be used as a crude measure of deterioration or improvement of the whole housing stock.

Prioritization and Programming

Prioritization of refurbishment projects can then be based on the remaining asset lives of like component assets or they can be area based with a project for total refurbishment or demolition/replacement. Development of the ensuing programmes is best carried out manually based on the information produced by the AMS. When initial appraisal is complete, the component functional or area-based projects are placed in the capital investment program alongside projects for new build. The timing of projects is determined within the investment program according to priorities and the availability of funding. Up to three versions of the investment program may be necessary:

- The set of projects which have commenced or are about to commence; this program is spread over the next two years and used to monitor progress and cash flow for financial purposes; it uses monthly data based on actual and predicted spend
- A five year program which shows the stage of approval of each imminent project so that they may be shepherded through the appraisal process; it uses quarterly data in the early years and biannual or annual in the latter years
- A long term (25 years is typical) program showing how projects are prioritised (based on objectives and targets) and smoothed to allow for a manageable use of resources; it will also allow for the long term planning of finance; data is presented in a yearly format

All three may use proprietary packages or simple spreadsheets.

Addendum 1 – 'A Decent Home'

There are four criteria (A, B, C and D) that make up the Decent Homes Standard. Many would consider them over-complex and somewhat confusing but that's typical of government publications as they are generally written by solicitors rather than practitioners. Consult the full document, which is available on the UK Government website, for details.

Criterion A: It meets the current statutory minimum standard for housing

Criterion B: It is in a reasonable state of repair

Criterion C: It has reasonably modern facilities and services

Criterion D: It provides a reasonable degree of thermal comfort

Hazard Profiles

The list which follows is taken from 'Housing Health and Safety Rating System', published online by the Office of the Deputy Prime Minister, Feb 2006. It forms the basis of a system to score risks associated with social housing (or any other set of buildings for that matter). It could be used to develop performance grades based on levels of service however it would seem to be sufficient (and less onerous) to simply check that all of the relevant issues have been included in the grading system.

Hygrothermal Conditions

- Damp and mould growth
- Excess cold
- Excess heat

Pollutants (non-microbial)

- Asbestos (and MMF)
- Biocides
- Carbon Monoxide and fuel combustion products
- Lead
- Radiation
- Uncombusted fuel gas
- Volatile Organic Compounds

Space, Security, Light and Noise

- Crowding and space
- Entry by intruders
- Lighting
- Noise

Hygiene, Sanitation and Water Supply

- Domestic hygiene, Pests and Refuse
- Food safety
- Personal hygiene, Sanitation and Drainage
- Water supply

Falls

- Falls associated with baths etc
- Falling on level surfaces etc
- Falling on stairs etc
- Falling between levels

Electric Shocks, Fires, Burns and Scalds

- Electrical hazards
- Fire
- Flames, hot surfaces etc

Collisions, Cuts and Strains

- Collision and entrapment
- Explosions
- Position and operability of amenities etc
- Structural collapse and falling elements

Addendum 2- Outline of an Asset Management Strategy for Social Housing

Writing a strategy from scratch is a daunting prospect, however, if presented with an example or a draft structure, the task immediately seems more manageable. The National Housing Federation produce a booklet: *Asset Management Repairs and Maintenance for Board Members*, October 2011 and this contains an appendix with a possible contents list. Whilst the list can be criticised, as rather long and somewhat repetitive, the topics are useful as an 'aide memoire'. In perusing this list, it becomes clear that Housing Managers consider 'Asset Management' to include all aspects of the management of the stock unlike most other businesses which confine its realm to capital refurbishment and replacement. Based on this listing, a proposed structure for a comprehensive *Housing Asset Management Strategy* is shown below:

Executive Summary

The Executive Summary should either be written in the name of the senior politician responsible for housing or there should be a short statement endorsing the report by them. The Summary should take up no more than two pages and should refer, in outline, to each of the main headings as well as highlighting particular problems and their proposed solutions. It may conclude with a few facts about the likely investment and the commitment for the future.

Introduction

The introduction should say why the report is being written, hence why a strategy is being produced and this will often refer to a recent problem which has prompted action to be taken. It may explain the main components of the strategy, referring briefly to stakeholder involvement, regulation and the review process, especially if this is not the first report on the subject.

Background

The background will refer to the regional and local housing situation, putting the subject of social housing into context with owner occupied property and other organisations which rent out property in the area. The local market and demand for rented property are key points. The need for asset management should be emphasised using the value of the stock to make the point.

Housing Strategy and the Corporate Plan

Presumably, a Corporate (or Business) Plan for the whole business is already in existence. The relationship between the Housing Strategy and the Corporate Plan should be explained (that the Housing Strategy is a Business Plan for that Department). This may include reference to Vision and Mission Statements for the whole organisation and for the department. Reference should be made to regulatory standards especially if published, such as the 'Decent Homes' standard. Reference may also be made to levels of customer satisfaction. Some explanation of the short-term (revenue) functions of operation and maintenance may be made in order to differentiate it from the (capital) Asset Management Plan.

The Existing Situation

Before explaining what needs to be done there should be a description of the existing stock, which may be based on the inventory used for the Asset Management Plan. Tables are more useful than text.

Gap Analysis

The demand is described, preferably in a similar form to that used to describe the existing stock. This can then be used to define the gap between the demand and the existing supply. The difference is the gap which has to be addressed. Deficiencies can be addressed under sub-headings:

- Repairs
- Refurbishment
- Disposal
- Demolition
- New build

Investment Programme

The investment programme is based on targets, i.e. specified needs which have to be met by a certain date. Some linkage between the demand/gap/target/project chain-of-events is useful. Explanation of the constituent schemes is also appreciated.

Clarity is crucial; therefore, it is important to differentiate between types of project in the investment programme. These would normally be appended in the form of spreadsheets.

- Those projects which are underway or about to start need detailed plans over the next year or two to enable financial control to be exerted.
- The main programme will normally be over five years exhibiting the stage of approval of each project which has a firm timescale
- A long term programme (normally over 25 years) that shows the expenditure profile which emerges from the Asset Management Plan.

Appendix 4

an AMS for Flood Defences

Background

Asset management (AM) was pioneered in New Zealand and Australia in the 1980s and has been adopted by a number of businesses in the UK. In particular it has featured heavily in OFWAT's regulation of the water industry in England and Wales where systems were standardized and methodologies refined. These procedures and systems have been used in many countries across the world enabling water (and other) undertakings to produce investment programs to look after their assets in the longer term. Whilst some have access to standards for compiling an AMS in their industry or country, many do not; this paper seeks to address that problem by providing a model for flood defences which can be developed further.

Introduction

There is a noticeable lack of consistency involving AM practices which have become commonplace in other industries. Research into the literature for AM in the area of flood defence reveals that there are systems and guidance notes and some organised methodology, however, the linkage between condition assessment and levels of service is rarely made. Assessment of the AMS used by the UK's Environment Agency:

http://www.environment- agency.gov.uk/research/policy/132948.aspx

who look after 55% of the relevant assets reveals that their system is based on three principles:

- Asset condition
- Reliability of operating plant
- Conveyance of channels

This would suggest that the link between condition and performance grades is not made, nor is there any attempt at valuation. PAS 55 and its big brother, ISO 55000, are not mentioned and would appear to play no part in the EA's AMS.

Assets maintained by third parties, which account for the remaining 45% are not subject to formal asset management procedures so a variety of systems will be in use or, in many cases, there is no system at all.

This paper is about adapting the basic principles of AM, as developed by the water industry in England and Wales, so that they may be easily adopted by anybody which is responsible for the management of flood defences leading to a prioritized investment programme as part of an asset management strategy.

How Asset Management Works

This is best illustrated in diagrams which show the interrelationship of the components centred on the asset inventory:

http://felixschrodinger.wordpress.com/2011/08/08/asset-management-presentation/

Slides 6 and 7 show the high level relationship of AM with other components of the management system and slide 29 shows a detailed view of how the inputs and outputs of the asset management system are centred on the inventory.

The inventory is normally a spreadsheet or simple database which includes all of the information relating to the assets to be included. The choice between databases and spreadsheets is a matter for the developer of the AMS but there are some things to consider. Spreadsheets are much easier to use especially during the data collection phase however they are not as good at selecting and sorting classes of asset for further consideration. In a database all records are locked as far as their data are concerned; if the order of the records is changed then all of the associated data will move with each relevant record automatically. This is not necessarily so for a spreadsheet and an unwary user can easily break the link between an asset and its associated data by moving things around in a table.

In the case of flood defences it is likely that separate tables will be required for differing types of asset, even though the processes will be the same. There will always be differences between structural and mechanical/electrical assets though these may be listed in a single table. However, land/building and transport/plant need separating. The inventory will normally consist of inputs including:

- Asset data
- Condition grades
- Performance grades based on 'levels of service'
- Asset lives
- Cost data

And will enable outputs:

- Prioritization for the investment program and strategies
- Current valuation
- Ad hoc reports

Each of these aspects will be discussed in some detail in the sections which follow.

Level of detail

Fundamental to the success of an AMS is the level of detail. We could choose to take a whole flood control system as a single asset but this would militate against practical management. On the other hand including too much detail takes excessive effort and can create confusion through lack of clarity.

A waterway must be assessed in two aspects: its sections by length (links), and features which exist at junctions (nodes). It difficult to design a single data table to suit both types of data so careful consideration must be given to how they are set up. A 'link' is a linear section and a 'node' is a junction or other point along the length of the asset where it is split into manageable sections. This concept is common to utilities which manage pipelines and cables but not so much in respect of waterway management. It is likely, therefore, due to differing data needs that that they will be best managed in separate inventories.

Linkage assets

First a watercourse must be defined in general (high level) terms and then split into manageable lengths which are based on a junction (confluence) or a change in the basic properties. A change in construction or profile is often selected as a node, however, it is suggested that links should not be excessive in length and artificial markers should be introduced if necessary. The following data is suggested in respect of each 'link' and 'node':

- Name of watercourse
- Left bank or right
- Unique identifier and/or descriptor (e.g. Tame + detailed location)
- 'Link' or 'node'*
- Type of waterway – e.g. main river, non-main, stream, dyke, ditch
- Start and end points (with grid references?)
- Construction – hard paved, earth bank, etc
- Length and width
- Builder/constructor
- Capacity (bank full) in m3/s
- Average and peak throughput
- Owner
- Maintainer

Each section of the waterway and component should have a unique identifier which should be self evident, for example: Tame/FB/17R/ would be the right flood bank of the River Tame, section 17.

Nodal assets

Information about nodes, which may be confluences or intermediate points along the length of the watercourse:

- Confluences (where water courses join)
- Bridges (which often restrict flow)
- Weirs

- Tunnels and Culverts
- Pump stations

The following information is then added for each individual asset:

- Name and reference number
- Asset status - in use or not (code: AB, NW, OP, UC)
- Condition grade (1-5)
- Performance grade (1-5)
- Year of construction/installation
- Asset life (in years)
- MEAV ($ replacement cost)
- Criticality (optional)
- Remarks

Status

Some inventories contain only assets which are in use. This is not quite right as even an abandoned asset has some value if only the residual land on which it resides. Codes are normally used: AB = abandoned; NW = not working; OP = operational/in use; UC = under construction. It is good practice to annotate anything which is not working with a comment in the 'remarks' column.

Condition Grading

Condition grading is based on what you see rather than how well the asset performs. It is not dependent upon how well it does its job as this is the role of the performance grade. The grades for various assets can be developed for them specifically or generic definitions can be used:

Grade	Description
1 – excellent	In 'as new' condition without even minor defects
2 – good	Minor defects only apparent and no major problems
3 – adequate	Some minor problems which do not affect overall performance and only occasional major problems
4 – poor	Significant issues on a regular basis which affect performance but do not affect safety overall
5 - awful	Significant problems which affect performance; unsafe

These grades are applicable, in general terms to most (non mechanical/electrical) assets and may be extended or replaced to deal with particular components where they already have specified condition grades. Where electrical components are present then the grades may be extended by adding a reference to electrical safety.

Sample condition grades for mechanical & electrical plant

CG	Grade	Asset Description
1	Excellent	• in 'as new' condition • electrically safe • requires only routine maintenance
2	Good	• shows only superficial signs of wear and tear, protective coatings still intact, no corrosion • electrically safe • infrequent minor failures
3	Adequate	• all components functioning well • significant signs of wear and tear, minor corrosion • electrically safe • regular minor failures but no major failures
4	Poor	• still functioning but requires substantial maintenance to be kept going • electrically safe but marginal • regular minor failures and occasional major failures
5	Awful	• frequent (monthly) breakdowns, not working or abandoned • electrically unsafe

Performance Grading

Performance grades are set based on defined levels of service criteria. Many organizations, including the EA, have confused this concept and have used the design criteria instead of the level of protection provided to the 'customer' (the one who's house or garden gets flooded). There is only one relevant performance grade for flooding and that is the level of protection afforded to buildings and property. This can be summarized using frequency of inundation as in the table below:

Grade	Description
1 – excellent	Frequency of flooding in buildings less than once in 1000 years and less than 100 years on adjacent land or highway
2 – good	Frequency of flooding in buildings less than once in 100 years and less than 50 years on adjacent land or highway
3 – adequate	Frequency of flooding in buildings less than once in 50 years and less than 20 years on adjacent land or highway
4 – poor	Frequency of flooding in buildings less than once in 20 years and less than 10 years on adjacent land or highway
5 - awful	Frequency of flooding in buildings more than once in 20 years or more than 10 years on adjacent land or highway

When Constructed and Asset Life

Each type of asset is accorded an asset life which is based on that experienced by typical assets in a similar environment. A set of standard asset lives is attached. The year of construction / installation is also required as a baseline for the asset life. Age is not used as it changes every year and is not, therefore, stable.

Replacement cost

There are many variations on the definition of the replacement cost but this will tend to be the cost of construction at the time of the survey. Some businesses use the 'Modern Equivalent Asset Value' (MEAV) concept which recognises that the replacement asset may be different from that originally built. Whichever is used, the replacement cost must be the full cost including all contract and administrative overheads. This can often increase the unit rate shown in a bill of quantities by a factor of more than two. The costing MUST be in a stable currency i.e. one with an inflation rate less than 10%. If in doubt use the USD.

Criticality

Many systems include a measure of risk assessment, often referred to as 'criticality'. Whilst useful this may not be essential as, in general, the bigger the asset, the more critical it will be. During the earlier years of the twenty first century, extreme rainfall caused flooding which threatened parts of the National Grid. If these installations were forced off-line, then parts of the country would suffer black-outs. A strategy to, identify and protect them was adopted. If a more sophisticated system is required see:

http://felixschrodinger.wordpress.com/2013/11/14/criticality/

Remarks

A remarks field is essential so that any data which is not normal can be explained. Reasons why a site has been abandoned are useful as the passage of time may mean that narrative is lost.

Output - RAL

The first output will be a calculation of the 'remaining asset life' (RAL). Some systems use simple percentages or even life in years based on the condition grade. This fails to recognise that performance is just as important; an undersized asset in perfect condition may require replacement because it is now under capacity. A typical 'look-up' table combining condition and performance is shown below. The RAL is calculated as a percentage RAL times the original asset life.

Condition Grade					
Performance Grade	1	2	3	4	5
1	100	87	75	62	50
2	87	75	62	50	37
3	75	62	50	37	25
4	62	50	37	25	12
5	50	37	25	12	1

Look-up Table showing the percentage remaining asset life (%RAL).

Output – Valuation

If the replacement cost (MEAV) is multiplied by the percentage remaining asset life, divided by 100 then we have the current asset value (CAV). This gives the current value of the asset but it is unlikely to include the value of the land on which it stands. This should be considered separately.

Prioritization

It remains to examine the asset, in areas or in groups, to determine which have the highest priority. This will include those with the shortest RAL and the highest criticality score (or the largest/most important). This is a task best done by human inspection and assessment based on the output from the AMS. Computers are not noted for their judgement in these matters. A set of projects, based on either area or asset type, can now be compiled and input to the capital investment program (CIP). Obviously this first attempt will not conform with the available funding profile or practical timescales. The program, which must also contain all new schemes, is then smoothed to take out peaks and troughs whilst allowing for available funding.

If your property is liable to flood, you can get useful information here:

https://felixschrodinger.wordpress.com/2014/02/16/the-gospel-according-to-noah/

Appendix 5

A Short Course in Asset Management

As this 'course' is based around a set of PowerPoint presentations, the detail is not included here. Following the links will take you to the presentation itself on-line.

Some authorities on the subject of Asset Management (AM) see it as an all-encompassing business model for any organisation which relies on physical assets to achieve its outputs; however others argue that it is solely concerned with the long-term maintenance of those assets in order to ensure that they continue to perform their allotted task:

http://felixschrodinger.wordpress.com/2010/11/13/asset-management-%E2%80%93-two-very-different-approaches/

This paper leaves the former approach to such esteemed publications as PAS 55:

http://felixschrodinger.wordpress.com/2011/08/09/the-requirements-of-pas-55/

and concentrates on latter. In this case Asset Management Planning (AMP) should be seen as that component of Capital Investment Programming (CIP) which applies to the existing assets; i.e. the task which a business carries out to decide where, when and how to invest capital in order to get continued return in income or provision of a service. Thus AM sits alongside: program management; project appraisal and strategic planning.

The asset management process

In roughly the following order, we require to undertake the following input tasks:

- Compile an asset inventory
- Carry out a survey and assign condition grades
- Compile a list of service grades -'levels of service' (LoS) based on customers' expectations
- Assign performance grades to each asset based on these LoS
- Assign asset lives

- Input asset replacement costs
- Assign criticality scores if required (optional)

And this may lead us to achieve outputs:

- Calculation of the remaining asset life for each asset
- A current valuation of the assets
- Priority listings for input to the investment program

The structure may be viewed in the diagram on page 4 in the presentation:

http://felixschrodinger.wordpress.com/2011/12/05/generic-resource-asset-management-system-gramps/

Each of these components must be considered in more detail starting with data collection and compilation of the inventory:

http://felixschrodinger.wordpress.com/2011/08/15/data-collection-and-referencing/

Following which we need to organise and carry out the condition survey:

http://felixschrodinger.wordpress.com/2011/08/11/condition-grading/

And then compile performance grades (not to be confused with 'performance indicators'), which need to be based on defined level of service criteria:

http://felixschrodinger.wordpress.com/2011/08/13/performance-grading/

Now we can add asset lives to the inventory:

http://felixschrodinger.wordpress.com/2011/08/10/asset-lives/

or:

http://felixschrodinger.wordpress.com/2013/11/01/standard-asset-lives/

Adding cost data will enable us to assess the current value of the asset base:

And we can include 'risk management' in the form of 'criticality' should we choose:

http://felixschrodinger.wordpress.com/2013/11/14/criticality/

Data inputs to the system are now complete and we will have chosen (at the beginning) to use some proprietary software to assist in data management. However will need to add some look-up tables to enable the remaining asset life (RAL) and current asset value to be calculated:

http://felixschrodinger.wordpress.com/2011/08/16/asset-valuation/

We may also use the RAL as a means to prioritize the schemes of refurbishment or replacement within the capital investment program (CIP):

http://felixschrodinger.wordpress.com/2011/08/03/capital-investment-program/

The projects which we compose (like a symphony!) will sit alongside or be consumed within other strategies:

http://felixschrodinger.wordpress.com/?s=strategic

and be subjected to the standard project appraisal procedures adopted by the business.

In summary we have a set of defined procedures, contained within logical methodology, leading to outputs which enable us to manage our assets for the future benefit of the business and our customers:

http://felixschrodinger.wordpress.com/2010/11/13/asset-management-planning-for-developing-countries/

Postscript: this 'course' is designed to run over two days but can be extended to four days over one week if each module is extended with practical exercises, using the collective experience of the attendees to enhance the learning experience.

Course Exercises

The basic course is designed to run over two days. If an extended course (say four days or 'day release') is required with the same content, then it may be reinforced with exercises. A classroom exercise is set up using a house (or 'home' if you prefer) as the subject, preferably with students using their own family home as the subject. The house is split into components and an inventory constructed using a spreadsheet. At each stage of the teaching process data is added to the example building up into an illustration of the complete process. A basis for this, for the course tutor, can be found at:

http://felixschrodinger.wordpress.com/2013/11/04/an-asset-management-system-for-social-housing/

The intention is to present the process of the AMS in practical terms which are easily identified with day-to-day experience. This exercise is intended to be completed, in stages, within the classroom and could be undertaken individually or in pairs.

A second type of exercise may be set in the form of a project which will be compiled as a report at the end of the course for marking. Once the outline of the subject (AM) is complete, students are asked to select an area for more detailed study which will become the subject of their project. It may be within their area of expertise or new to them. Any asset-rich business or utility will suffice but here are some suggestions:

- An airport
- A fleet (e.g. transport, mobile plant, aircraft, ships etc.)
- A water or wastewater treatment plant
- A power station
- A pipe or cable network

- A property portfolio
- Government buildings

As each week goes by the learned material is adapted to the subject and added to the project building up to a valuation and the compilation of a prioritized investment program. After (say) one month, a final report is produced for marking.

At all stages, collaboration between the students should be encouraged and they should be required to present sections of their work as the course proceeds. When the reports are complete a final presentation session should be held followed by a course appraisal.

Appendix 6

Asset Management Planning for Developing Countries

Abstract

The built environment consists not only of buildings but also of the essential support infrastructure such as highways and utility services. These assets frequently fail because of inadequate maintenance and investment as they reach the end of their useful lives. Only with a system for the replacement of assets, when they become obsolete or beyond reasonable repair, can those responsible ensure the effectiveness and efficiency of their businesses. The methods employed in asset management have much in common with the accountants" approach to depreciation but differ significantly in that condition and performance are the prime drivers rather than age and fixed asset lives. The setting up of an asset management system is well within the capabilities of any organization and much time and effort can be saved if the tasks are dealt with in a structured manner. Thus the primary tasks can be organized into a sequence involving: inventory compilation, grading and costing. The resulting information can then be used to provide a valuation of tangible assets and forms the basis to drive the rehabilitation and replacement aspects of a capital investment program.

The Meaning and Objective of Asset Management

Whilst the term "asset management" may have different meanings to many people, its meaning in the context of the constructed environment is simple: "to ensure, through refurbishment or replacement, the continued delivery of intended outputs to the beneficiaries of those outputs". The receivers of the benefits are often referred to as "customers" though in the case of a building they may be occupiers or tenants.

Asset management is not about the short term maintenance of assets which is a regular process concerned with keeping the asset in functioning condition for the operators. Nor is it concerned with the day-to-day management of the assets i.e. facilities management.

The External Context

Funding agencies, who bankroll much construction in developing countries, have recognized that, with finite resources, they cannot continue to pour unlimited funds into the premature replacement of neglected assets. This view is well founded and along with the concept of 'appropriate technology' coincides with the new morality of only providing that which can be sustainably managed thus avoiding problems for the next generation. There are many others who have a part to play in ensuring that constructions are sustainable. **Fig 1** shows the players in relationship to each other and the investment programme. It also introduces the asset inventory which forms the basis of asset management planning.

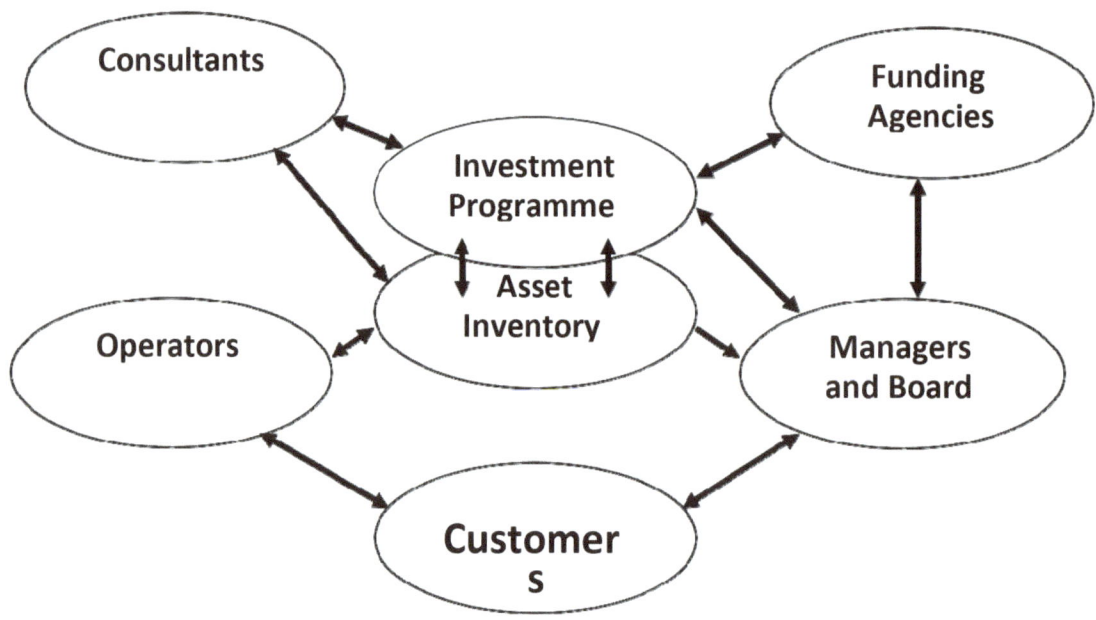

Fig 1 Stakeholders in the Built Environment

The term 'customers' is used to denote those who benefit from the output of, or use of, the constructed asset(s).

The Internal Context

An asset management plan needs to be administered and placed within a structure which is organized to deliver the planned benefits to the intended 'customers'. These 'capital' functions, which relate to the spending of funds, include:

- Strategic planning
- Asset management planning
- Project appraisal
- Investment programme management

Whilst some of the detailed tasks may be contracted out (e.g. to consultants), all of them must be present and effective for the outputs of a construction programme to be sustainable. The more advanced processes (especially design, tendering and construction) are normally outsourced.

The need for an asset management plan (AMP) is most evident in those areas where maintenance and rehabilitation have been neglected resulting in a lower level of service to customers. Where the care of buildings and operational plant is not properly managed, early renewal becomes the only option to abandonment. Thus heavy (re)investment is undertaken by funding agencies often on a (roughly) ten year cycle and little is done locally between interventions.

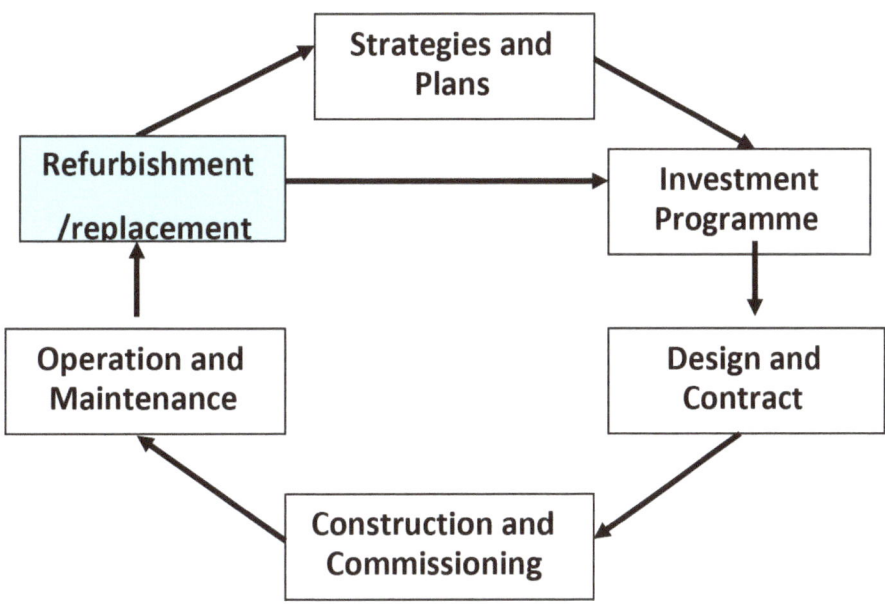

Fig 2 asset management covers replacement / refurbishment within the construction cycle.

Asset management looks after the replacement and refurbishment of the assets by planning to keep them in operation before they wear out. Thus it can easily be seen to be an essential part of any sustainable system in the life of infrastructure - build only that which you can look after and then look after it.

Benefits

The benefits of an AMP can be listed:

- Provides a central inventory with unique references
- Provides consistent information on capacity, throughput, condition etc.
- Links investment with service levels through performance grades
- Provides a valuation of tangible assets
- Plans and prioritizes investment
- Can be used to measure and record improvement

Whilst these are not detailed here one can see immediate benefits such as the ability to feed consultants and project planners with up-to-date asset information.

Outline of the Methodology

An AMP consists mainly of an inventory of assets - usually contained in a database - and a computerized system that aids valuation and compiles output in such a way that the priorities for investment can easily be recognized and acted upon. **Fig 3** shows the typical layout of an AMP and the interaction of the components.

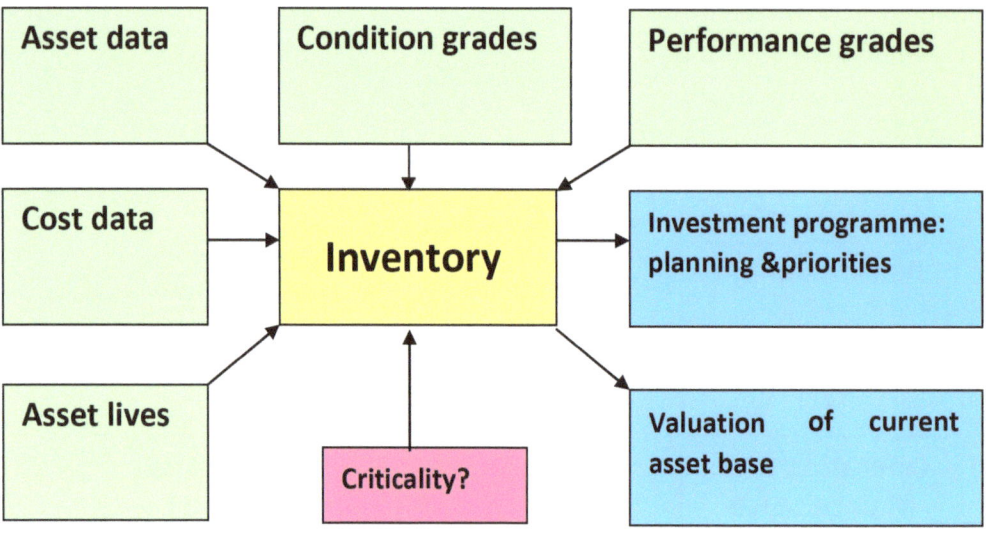

Typical AMP structure

The methodology involves firstly compiling a set of databases and spreadsheets - the inventory of all tangible assets. The most important assets will vary according to the nature of the business of the organization, thus for a water utility they would include dams, boreholes, treatment plants pump stations and pipelines but for a power company it would be generating plants, sub stations and power lines. A rail operator would wish to list lines, stations, goods yards and rolling stock.

After setting up a basic inventory the next stage involves assessing the condition of the assets, following this performance is assessed, and thirdly replacement costs are estimated. When these data are complete the condition and performance grades are compared with a look-up table and a percentage remaining asset life (RAL) is assigned. This, multiplied by the replacement cost gives the current asset value (CAV). The condition and performance grades, with the nominal asset life, can then be used to assign priority to the assets for replacement or refurbishment.

The remaining part of this paper is concerned with more detailed advice on setting up an asset management plan based on the author's TRAMP system developed for use by a water utility in the Caribbean.

Inventories

The organisation of the asset inventory is crucial to the success and efficiency of the planning process. Trying to put all of the data for an organisation (large or small) into a single inventory is fraught with difficulties. The data to be stored are so varied that a single table or set of related tables may soon become over complex and littered with empty fields. Whilst the data can be collected into a series of spreadsheets, there are considerable benefits in using a database which allows sorting and filtering to be done much more easily.

Data can be collected at three levels:

- plant or location level (one entry per site)
- process level (typically 10 entries per site)
- unit level (typically 100 entries per site)

Using a water utility as an example, the plant level would consist of a water treatment plant being considered as a single entry. The process level would take each part of the plant which performs a different process separately. At the unit level each pump, screen, channel etc. is included individually. The choice of the level to be used is crucial to data efficiency. The upper level is too crude and the lower level too detailed thus the middle level is normally recommended. Each component process is included in the inventory and separately graded.

As will be seen later in Section 3, it is also necessary to differentiate between structures and mechanical/electrical components as they have very different asset lives and often exhibit very different condition grades.

Organization

The development of a relational database may be beyond the means of many small organisations. There are therefore two approaches that can be taken:

- build up a single set of related tables in one inventory
- organize the data into separate types so that a series of "flat file" tables are created

In the initial stages of development the latter option is by far the simplest to adopt and this is recommended. If, at a later stage, a relational database is required then it can be compiled relatively quickly as the problems concerned with the data collection and storage will, by then, have been resolved.

Any organisation will tend to have different types of asset. The typical division of data types, this time using an airport as an example, is given below:

- Land
- Taxiways
- Traffic control
- Fuelling facilities
- Miscellaneous e.g. vehicles, furniture, computers etc.

- Runway
- Terminals
- Other buildings
- Mobile plant
- Safety and security assets

Data collection

Data collection is a classic 'chicken and egg' conundrum. How do you know what to collect until you've tried? The resolution of this problem involves the development of the methodology first, then the use of test data to debug it. This will give a practical solution quickly but not the final structure; a database should be seen as a living entity and subject to further refinement.

The preferred process is to define an objective methodology and then collect data, at first subjectively and then objectively. In practice data collection tends to be undertaken before the methodology has been defined as this is the easiest thing to do and progress will be apparent even if the whole exercise has to be repeated. The use of a small sample of test data results in a robust system being reached quickly.

The primary entries can be set up from existing tables of assets, where they are available, and the principle exercises of correlation will be based on getting information from previous reports, system maps and from field operators.

Each of the organisation's functional areas will have existing data to be compiled as the basis of the inventory and there will be gaps, duplications and errors. The key to correcting these errors involves firstly cross-checking the data of the master sets against each other. Secondly a system of "partial publication", to interested parties, is undertaken with selected areas highlighted for them to check. As each stage of data collection is completed the draft table is circulated to field operatives and corrections are requested. During this process most duplications and omissions are quickly picked up and the use of multiple names can be rationalised.

The procedure for compiling an AMP is listed below:

1. collect all existing data on systems and assets
2. structure database tables and headings
3. collect sample condition grade data
4. test database with sample data and design input formats (forms)
5. undertake condition grade assessments (site surveys) and compile database
6. develop levels of service (LoS) standards
7. undertake performance grading with operational staff and enter data
8. input asset lives
9. input cost data
10. design queries and output reports
11. run valuation and prioritization reports

Data Fields

A database requires that data fields be defined before storage can take place. The simplest guide to the likely field requirements is to look at the existing data sets or examples that have been produced elsewhere. It is simple to spot the recurring data requirements involving references, names, location, size, material, type, etc. These form the basic set up for the data tables and are revised once the initial system is compiled. At this stage the best way to debug the tables is to use a set of test data involving at least ten records.

Hardware and Software

The issue of hardware is now fairly simple as the preferred solution will always be to use the simplest system capable of doing the job. A single PC with an A3 colour printer is normally quite sufficient.

The wide availability of M/S Windows makes it a suitable platform and both XL and Access may be used in compiling the asset inventory.

There also exists, at this point, an obvious opportunity for a commercial or academic organization to build an on-line system which can be remotely accessed from anywhere in the world. Whilst the major benefit would ensue from providing clients with a readymade system, the greatest advantages could ensue from the parent organisation's ability to use the data for research. Such a development could also be of great benefit to the funding agencies in being able to collect data in a standardised format.

Condition Grading

Condition Grades (CG's) are simply a consideration and recording of the soundness of an asset in terms of wear and tear. 'Condition' describes its structural integrity and safety, and is therefore that which can be seen. CGs do not take into account the performance of the item as performance grades are assigned separately. A sample grading structure is appended.

Survey

Condition grading is normally best undertaken by a team of two persons - one who is responsible for data collection and one who operates and maintains the assets on a daily basis. This ensures both local input and consistency. Simple forms are used to gather the information.

Condition grades for buried assets (e.g. cables and pipelines) are more difficult to assess initially and the first set of grades may be have to be subjectively applied. These are gradually improved as failure data, and survey information, linked to assets or areas, becomes available.

Grades

Each asset identified in the inventory must be given a condition grade. In the case of assets which consist of structural and mechanical/electrical (M&E) parts two grades are required. The basic grading system is simple and must be used consistently to aid comparisons with others:

Grade	Description
1	Excellent
2	Good
3	Adequate
4	Poor
5	Awful

Basic grading system

Grades of 1 to 5 ranging from excellent (1) to awful (5) are assigned. To get a meaningful profile the grades must reflect the full range of assets. The appendix shows a more detailed description of typical generic condition grades.

Performance Grading

Performance grades (PGs) are a measure of how well an asset performs its allotted task and will reflect its reliability; it is not a measure of how new it is. Nor is it a measure against the specification but a grading against the required output **as perceived by the customer**. Assets can be in excellent condition but are not achieving the required output and vice versa. This is particularly true in the case of inappropriate technology (i.e. the wrong tool for the job).

In order to perform this task properly it is necessary, first, to define the "levels of service" (LoS) that the customers receive or expect to receive. Thus grade 1 (excellent) represents the aspiration of the organization and grade 5 (awful) the lowest level of service that is supplied to a significant population.

A single PG will suffice for each asset/process, there being no need to differentiate between a structure and M&E components.

Levels of Service

The "performance" must be assessed or graded against a set of defined criteria or "levels of service". These are set in relation to customer perceived performance rather than against abstract design criteria - in simple terms - i.e. does it do the job?

Thus, performance will reflect the loading, configuration and type of unit being employed and not its condition. A LoS scheme for a railway company could include:

- Punctuality
- Availability capacity
- Frequency of service
- Safety in transit

To allow a reasonable spread of occurrences within the grades the performance definitions should take account of the local situation.

Grades

Grades are assigned within the same general approach - ranging from excellent (1) to awful (5) - as for condition. Again performance is assessed at the process level though a whole plant may be given a single grade at first and then refined as the information improves. Thus passenger delays at an airport could be graded 4 but on subsequent examination it is determined that the baggage handling system is to blame for the problem and the grade is then assigned to that process to reflect this.

Performance grading is undertaken between asset management staff and the managers responsible for the assets' operation. This ensures that consistency is maintained. An example of LoS for power supply is given below:

CS1	Continuous Supply
CS2	Supply for 100 hours per week
CS3	Supply for 50 hours per week
CS4	Supply for 25 hours per week
CS5	Supply less than 25 hours per week

Sample level of service criteria

Valuation

The valuation process is based on the replacement cost or 'modern equivalent asset value' (MEAV). This is reduced to a percentage of its full value according to the condition and performance of the asset to give the current asset value (CAV).

Asset Lives

The first step in the valuation process is to add the asset lives to the inventory. Typically structures will last 50-60 years and M&E plant about fifteen. A list of asset values, based on those used by the accountants, is developed for use in calculations within the database.

Modern Equivalent Asset Value (MEAV)

The inventory itself will not yet provide the valuation of the assets necessary for business purposes. In order to achieve this it will be necessary to add cost data for each type of asset. The replacement cost is used and it this can be based on size bands for the type of asset. The MEAV represents the cost of replacing the asset with an equivalent one that is capable of performing the required task and is thus based on throughput rather than capacity.

This same cost data can be used both in the valuation and, later in an investment programme as the first estimate for budget purposes. It is also useful in strategy development as the basis for appraisal of options. The values are based on cost curves or matrices as is most appropriate for each type of asset and are updated annually in a stable currency.

Remaining Asset Life

The remaining asset life (RAL) is calculated as a percentage from a look-up table contained within the database. A typical example is shown below:

Condition Grade

Perf. Grade	1	2	3	4	5
1	100	75	50	25	10
2	85	65	40	20	7
3	70	50	30	15	4
4	60	40	20	10	2
5	50	30	10	5	1

Percentage Remaining Asset Life (%RAL)

Current Asset Value (CAV)

Calculating the current asset value is now simply a matter of multiplying the MEAV by the

%RAL, e.g:

 Say MEAV = $100,   Condition grade 4   Performance grade 3

Refer to Condition / performance matrix for %RAL

Remaining Asset Life = 15% therefore

CAV = 100 x 0.15 = $15

The database is configured to provide a report which summarises the replacement and current values thus giving a statement of the organisation's assets in operational terms for comparison with the book values contained in the accounts.

Rehabilitation and Renewal

The next step is to use the information gathered in order to be able to give priorities for renewal and refurbishment to all projects. Similar assets may be grouped into action plans for improvement or areas may be chosen for levels of service improvements. These should all be part of documented strategies.

6.1 Priorities and Investment Program drivers

The prioritization of rehabilitation schemes can be set up, initially using the remaining asset lives:

- Calculate Remaining Asset Life (RAL) in years

$$RAL(yrs) = AL(yrs) \times \%RAL /100$$

- Produce provisional priority listing based on RAL (in ascending order)

This can be further refined if assets have been assigned a 'criticality index', which represents the importance of the asset within the overall system, however, in most cases, it is valid to assume that the assets with the greatest throughput will be the most critical. All that remains is to cross check which assets are already contained within projects, action plans or other initiatives:

- Annotate projects with project or strategy names
- Allocate remaining projects to the investment programme or to new action plans as part of overall strategy

Planning for the future

Long term planning may now be undertaken using the information from the database and associated strategies. Using the remaining asset lives, crude estimates of renewal rates can be produced as a basis (no more) for predicting annual expenditure on renewal and refurbishment. This, with prioritization of the investment programme, represents the next phase of development.

Conclusions

An asset management plan is essential for the long term sustainability of any group of constructed assets.

Whilst there is expensive proprietary software available, a simple system can be set up using a PC and a simple database. The methodology described can be adapted by any organisation or business for its own use.

It is not necessary to specify all of the requirements before commencing work; a gradual development involving the users of the data is preferred. Subjective judgements of grades may be made initially and later replaced with objective data based on measurement and observation.

To be effective, both condition and the performance of assets (based on levels of service) should be recorded.

The generic grades (1=excellent to 5=awful) are fundamental and must not be altered, however, the detailed grade descriptions should be amended to reflect the local environment and levels of service.

Research into the reasons for asset failure would be useful to determine the reasons why asset management is not universally understood and employed. With this understanding the sustainability of the constructed environment may, hopefully, be improved.

The time may now be opportune to create an easy-to-use, on-line asset management system within an academic or commercial organization concerned with the sustainability of the built environment.

Addendum

Sample condition grades for mechanical & electrical plant

CG	Grade	Asset Description
1	Excellent	• in 'as new' condition • electrically safe • requires only routine maintenance
2	Good	• shows only superficial signs of wear and tear, protective coatings still intact, no corrosion • electrically safe • infrequent minor failures
3	Adequate	• all components functioning well • significant signs of wear and tear, minor corrosion • electrically safe • regular minor failures but no major failures
4	Poor	• still functioning but requires substantial maintenance to be kept going • electrically safe but marginal • regular minor failures and occasional major failures
5	Awful	• frequent (monthly) breakdowns, not working or abandoned • electrically unsafe

Appendix 7
GRAMS

GRAMS (GeneRic Asset Management System) is a simple system which is designed to enable any business or utility to look after its physical assets. It has many potential applications:

- highways and associated structures
- water pipelines and plant
- gas pipeline and plant
- telecoms and TV networks and plant
- electricity networks and plant
- building complexes e.g. universities, film studios, offices
- transport fleets, road, rail sea and air
- rail track and stations
- docks and harbours
- airports
- rivers and flood defences
- waterways
- land, farming, forestry and woodland
- national parks
- local authority assets
- manufacturing plants e.g. motor, chemical, aircraft
- waste management sites and plant
- military establishments
- military hardware, land sea and air

It would enable any business to undertake key tasks which can include:

- asset inventories including links, nodes and sites
- condition grading
- performance grading
- replacement and current valuation of assets
- suggested remedial measures
- prioritisation of capital investment

- compilation of a capital investment programme
- links to maintenance schedules

The key drivers for wishing to compile an asset management system (AMS) include:

- long term planning of asset replacements
- valuation of the fixed assets within a business
- prioritisation and planning
- monitoring of the overall asset condition and performance against time
- maintaining a comprehensive asset inventory as a base for other users

GRAMS consists of a number of modules which can serve, or are served by, the inventory. This database consists of a record of all links, nodes and sites which are owned by, or used by the organisation. It is constructed in an M/S Access database. Links consist of one dimensional assets such as pipes, cables, ducts, stretches of highway etc. Nodes are junctions between links, changes in type of conduit and small items of plant which are situated along the networks.

Sites are complex facilities which may consist of buildings and processes. Examples include: waterworks; power stations; airport terminals; factories; buildings etc. Sites are divided further into individual processes so that they may be considered separately and each may be graded

Due to the inherent differences in the data types, the data on links, nodes and sites are kept in separate inventories within the database.

The inventories themselves are built in such a way that they can be used for any type of asset and any industry or business undertaking. The basis for this is the use of non- industry specific terms such as: 'condition'; 'performance'; 'grade'; replacement cost; 'asset life' etc.

In order to customise the application to a particular industry, a set of supporting documentation is required which would consist of:

- industry specific referencing codes (unique identifiers)
- customer levels of service and related performance grades
- details of condition grades (based on generic descriptions)
- asset lives
- asset replacement costs

Performance and Condition Grades

1	Excellent
2	Good
3	Adequate
4	Poor
5	Awful

The above table provides the generic description for the performance and condition grades which should never be altered. Some organisations cannot bring themselves to use the word 'awful' and so have adopted the term 'very poor'. Some have reversed the system using 5 as 'excellent' and 1 as 'awful'; this is a fundamental mistake as it puts the whole system in opposition to international practice.

Each performance grade (PG) is supported by a list of 'Levels of Service' (LoS) criteria as they apply to the recipient of the service (the 'customer'). Each condition grade (CG) is supported by a detailed description of the criteria or, in some cases, by typical photographs to illustrate the grades.

These grades can be used within a simple matrix to define the remaining asset life (RAL) and this can be used as a basis for further development.

Remaining Asset Life

The RAL is calculated as a percentage, based on a look-up table:

		Condition Grade				
		1	2	3	4	5
Performance Grade	1	100	87	75	62	50
	2	87	75	62	50	37
	3	75	62	50	37	25
	4	62	50	37	25	12
	5	50	37	25	12	1

The table above is indicative of assets where the condition and performance rank equally. For some types of asset, however this may not be the case; for instance, a pump may be in excellent condition (grade 1) but performing badly (grade 5) because it is the wrong type of pump. The RAL in this case would probably be more than 50%, however in the reverse situation (CG5 and PG1) the value would be less than 50%. The value of a pipeline is also less than obvious; regardless of the condition, its value reduces significantly once it reaches PG4 or 5. Some thought must be applied to the values in the table relating them to the type of asset and the relationship between performance and condition. The RAL is then used to calculate:

- the actual remaining life in years if combined with the asset life
- the current value of the asset (CAV) if combined with the replacement cost
- the priority for action, especially if combined with a number representing the criticality of the asset (typically the throughput).

These secondary items provide the basis for capital planning, depreciation calculations and valuation. Prioritisation of schemes is best carried out manually rather than using software.

Appendix 8

Procedures

The procedures which follow are designed to list the necessary steps in a simple sequence. They are offered on an advisory basis in a format which is designed to be printed out, two sided on A4 paper. Whilst most are relevant to water assets, they may be easily adapted to other businesses.

- The AMP framework
- Compiling the plant inventory
- Compiling the pipelines inventory
- Condition grading
- Performance grading
- Assigning cost data
- Capital programming
- Scheme appraisal
- Strategy development
- Demand forecasting
- Distribution strategy
- Sewerage strategy

Function:	Asset Management	Ref.	AMP/10

Procedure:	AMP Framework

Author:	PWS	Manager:	SA

Created:	01/09/xx	Updated:	

Status:	Draft

Purpose and Scope

This procedure lays down the steps to be taken to ensure that an effective Asset Management Plan is set up. It is relevant to all plant and pipelines that are under the control of the asset owner.

Responsibility

The Deputy General Manager (Operations) is responsible for the production of this procedure, its updating and implementation. [CLIENT] will be responsible for ensuring that the steps contained are complied with.

Procedure

- Identify area of coverage and outline range of plant, pipelines and problems
- Define scope of the Asset Management Plan (AMP)
- Set draft Levels of Service (LoS) criteria
- Define Condition (CGs) and Performance Grades (PGs)
- Determine level of plant detail required and design plant inventory
- Design pipeline inventory
- Compile inventories (AMP/3 & 4)
- Agree LoS criteria and grading system
- Survey plants and assess CGs (AMP/6)
- Interview operators and assess PGs (AMP/7)
- Complete other essential inventory data
- Produce initial grading and valuation reports
- Set up Purpose and Priority Codes
- Produce prioritized listing for strategy development and entry of schemes into CIP (AMP/12)
- Operate continuous data improvement system (AMP/5); update gradings and plant information according to:
  - strategies and action plans
  - new plant

- better information from operators
- measured service levels

Related Procedures

This procedure should be read in conjunction with the following procedures which are relevant to satisfactory completion of the process:

- AMP/3 & 4   Compiling the Inventories
- AMP/11   Operator input to the CIP
- AMP/12   Investment identification and prioritization
- AMP/16   Scheme appraisal
- AMP/17   Reporting
- AMP/19   Strategic development

Function:	Asset Management	Ref.	AMP/3

Procedure:	Compiling the Plant Inventory

Author:	PWS	Manager:	SA

Created:	29/5/xx	Updated:	

Status:	Draft

Purpose and Scope

This procedure lays down the steps to be taken for the orderly compilation of the plant inventory. It applies to all assets whether planned, in service or abandoned.

Responsibility

The Deputy General Manager (Operations) is responsible for the production of this procedure, its updating and implementation. [CLIENT] will be responsible for ensuring that the steps contained are complied with.

Procedure

- Identify key personnel and contact with explanation of task
- Investigate existing data sources and collect originals or copies
- Examine data and identify key items, desirable items and 'surplus to requirements' data
- Consult operator and collect available data
- Consult responsible manager and agree key data items and referencing system
- Construct draft data table format and enter test data
- Consult with interested parties
- Proceed with data collection and entry
- Amend structure according to feedback
- Add Condition Grades from survey
- Print out data sets and send to responsible managers for amendment
- Update inventory and feedback to data providers, copy to Responsible Manager
- Add draft Performance Grades and Replacement Values
- Copy data and gradings to Operator with request to check and amend
- Update inventory and feedback data sets to interested parties
- Publish completed data sets in appropriate form to all interested parties, request notification of mistakes, updates etc. as and when they occur

- Audit regular use of data and requirements to amend the structure when inventory is in regular use, record for annual update
- After twelve months circulate data sets for amendment and make request for details of any additional data fields that are required
- Update inventory based on responses

Definitions

"interested parties"   Asset owner, [CLIENT] Managers, the Operator, Consultants, Survey Contractors, etc.

"inventory"   The tables of data contained in the Access database managed by [CLIENT]

Related Procedures

This procedure should be read in conjunction with the following procedures which are relevant to satisfactory completion of the process:

- AMP/4   Updating data in the inventory
- AMP/5   Condition grading
- AMP/6   Performance grading
- AMP/7   Assigning cost data

Function:	Asset Management	Ref.	AMP/4

Procedure:	Compiling the Pipeline Inventory

Author:	PWS	Manager:	SA

Created:	30/5/xx	Updated:	

Status:	Draft

Purpose and Scope

This procedure lays down the steps to be taken for the orderly compilation of the inventory of pipeline assets. It covers all existing water pipelines and all new water and sewer pipelines as they are handed over to the asset owner.

Responsibility

The Deputy General Manager (Operations) is responsible for the production of this procedure, its updating and implementation. [CLIENT] will be responsible for ensuring that the steps contained are complied with.

Procedure

- Survey Contractor produces system maps and GIS input files
- Operator compiles system records in GIS
- Data tables designed by [CLIENT] in Access and agreed with Operator
- Operator provides test output of data in digital format
- Inventory adjusted to accept data and verified that transfer is working
- Programme of data transfer agreed
- Data transferred as and when available according to program
- [CLIENT] feedback faults to Operator for correction
- Operator supplies corrected data
- [CLIENT] enters draft condition and performance grades
- Condition and performance grades submitted to Operator for feedback
- [CLIENT] amends gradings and enters cost data
- Inventory ready for use in Capital program
- New water mains added as they are accepted by the asset owner
- Sewers added as they are accepted by the asset owner
- System and data audited every twelve months
- Improvements to format and data implemented

Related Procedures

This procedure should be read in conjunction with the following procedures which are relevant to satisfactory completion of the process:

- AMP/3   Compiling the Plant Inventory
- AMP/5   Updating data
- AMP/6   Condition grading
- AMP/7   Performance grading

Function:	Asset Management	Ref.	AMP/6

Procedure:	Condition grading

Author:	PWS	Manager:	SA

Created:	29/06/xx	Updated:	

Status:	Draft

Purpose and Scope

This procedure lays down the steps to be taken for the orderly condition grading of plant and pipelines. It covers all existing assets (plant and pipelines) and new ones as they are handed over to the asset owner.

Responsibility

The Deputy General Manager (Operations) is responsible for the production of this procedure, its updating and implementation. [CLIENT] will be responsible for ensuring that the steps contained are complied with.

Procedure (plant)

- Produce printout of data table with fields to cover condition grading
- Produce plant input sheets, blank if new survey, with old data if already surveyed
- Schedule inspections with Operator and agree program
- Inspect sites, fill in or amend survey sheets
- Assign unit condition grades based on detailed definitions and agree
- Assign overall grades for Structure and M&E and agree
- Operator adds detailed grades to plant maintenance system
- [CLIENT] adds overall grades to inventory
- Inventory copied to Operator for confirmation and file

Procedure (pipelines)

- Produce printout of data table with fields to cover condition grading
- Enter grade 3 in all fields as default
- Examine listing for new pipelines and amend to grade 1 or 2 as appropriate
- Copy DMA/SDA listing from Operator with bursts data
- Discuss LoS problems, based on bursts, with Operator where definitive data not available
- Assess all strategic pipelines individually

- Identify problem areas and grade as 4 or 5 as appropriate based on burst frequency
- Amend gradings in inventory for problem areas
- Print out table with condition grades by DMA/SDA
- Circulate to Operator and asset owner staff for comment
- Amend as appropriate following feedback

Related Procedures

This procedure should be read in conjunction with the following procedures which are relevant to satisfactory completion of the process:

- AMP/3   Compiling the Plant Inventory
- AMP/4   Compiling the Pipeline Inventory
- AMP/5   Updating data
- AMP/7   Performance grading

Function:	Asset Management	Ref.	AMP/7

Procedure:	Performance grading

Author:	PWS	Manager:	SA

Created:	29/08/xx	Updated:	

Status:	Draft

Purpose and Scope

This procedure lays down the steps to be taken for the orderly performance grading of plant and pipelines. It covers all existing assets (plant and pipelines) and new ones as they are handed over to the asset owner.

Responsibility

The Deputy General Manager (Operations) is responsible for the production of this procedure, its updating and implementation. [CLIENT] will be responsible for ensuring that the steps contained are complied with.

Procedure (plant)

- Produce printout of plant data table with fields to cover performance grading
- Collect LoS data from Operator, Municipality and any other sources
- Use data collation sheet to assign plant performance grades based on detailed definitions
- Provide copy of draft gradings on collation sheet to Operator for feedback
- Amend and complete collation sheet based on feedback
- [CLIENT] adds grades to inventory
- Inventory copied to Operator for confirmation and file

Procedure (pipelines)

- Produce printout of data table by DMA/SDA with fields to cover performance grading
- If first assessment enter grade 3 in all fields as default
- Examine listing for new or nearly new pipelines and amend to grade 1 or 2 as appropriate
- Copy DMA/SDA listing from Operator with performance data
- Discuss LoS problems, based on continuity, pressure and quality (flooding and interruptions for sewers) with Operator where definitive data not available
- Assess all strategic pipelines individually
- Identify problem areas and grade as 4 or 5 as appropriate based on LoS provided

- Amend gradings in inventory for problem areas
- Print out table with condition grades sorted by DMA/SDA
- Circulate to Operator and asset owner staff for comment
- Amend as appropriate following feedback

Related Procedures

This procedure should be read in conjunction with the following procedures which are relevant to satisfactory completion of the process:

- AMP/3   Compiling the Plant Inventory
- AMP/4   Compiling the Pipeline Inventory
- AMP/5   Updating data
- AMP/6   Condition grading

Attached

Plant data collation sheet

Function:	Asset Management	Ref.	AMP/8

Procedure:	Assigning cost data

Author:	PWS	Manager:	SA

Created:	01/09/xx	Updated:	

Status:	Draft		

Purpose and Scope

This procedure lays down the steps to be taken for the orderly assignment of cost data for plant and pipelines. It covers all existing assets (plant and pipelines) and new ones as they are handed over to the asset owner.

Responsibility

The Deputy General Manager (Operations) is responsible for the production of this procedure, its updating and implementation. [CLIENT] will be responsible for ensuring that the steps contained are complied with.

Procedure (plant)

- Produce printout of data table, sorted by 'Use', with 'MEAV' and 'Capacity' fields
- Produce up to date copy of the relevant plant cost table for the plant type (Use)
- Look up cost in $US for the plant throughput in l/s, interpolate between nearest values and divide between 'Structure' and 'M&E'
- Enter cost values onto printout or direct to inventory, check data and update inventory
- Repeat for each plant type
- *Go to 'Forms' and scroll through main form with cursor on 'CAV'*
- Check valuation summary report is producing correct output
- Print out required tables and reports and back up data

Procedure (pipelines)

- Produce data table, on screen, with MEAV and size fields
- Sort by size
- Produce up to date copy of the relevant pipeline cost tables
- For each size enter the default value in all vacant entries as $US per metre in MEAV
- Overwrite any previous default entries
- Check default values are complete

- Where entries are bespoke use data tables to provide current value and amend if necessary
- Check table for completeness
- *Run calculation using main form with cursor on 'CAV' field*
- Check Summary Valuation Report to see that valuations are properly calculated
- Print out required tables and reports and back up data

Related Procedures

This procedure should be read in conjunction with the following procedures which are relevant to satisfactory completion of the process:

- AMP/3   Compiling the Plant Inventory
- AMP/4   Compiling the Pipeline Inventory
- AMP/5   Updating data
- AMP/6   Condition grading
- AMP/7   Performance grading

Definitions

"MEAV"   Modern Equivalent Asset Value - the current full replacement cost

"CAV"   Current asset value

Function:	Asset Management	Ref.	AMP/15

Procedure:	Capital Programming

Author:	PWS	Manager:	SA

Created:	3/06/xx	Updated:	

Status:	Draft

Purpose and Scope

This procedure lays down the steps to be taken to ensure that the Capital Investment program is run efficiently and effectively. It is relevant to all plant and pipeline investments of the program that are under the control of the asset owner.

Responsibility

The Deputy General Manager (Operations) is responsible for the production of this procedure, its updating and implementation. [CLIENT] will be responsible for ensuring that the steps contained are complied with.

Procedure

- Design overall framework of Program Management to include: schemes, costs, timing, responsibilities, gradings, beneficiaries, purpose codes, priorities and criticality
- Identify investment needs including Operator input (AMP/11) and scheme priorities (AMP/12)
- Enter schemes from Strategies (AMP/19-22)
- Draw up CIP listing on computer
- Cost schemes (AMP/14)
- Produce draft expenditure profile
- Consult funding agencies
- Adjust program and reprofile
- Produce CIP and obtain approval to profile and funding requirements
- Obtain approval of the funding agencies to borrowing requirements
- Proceed with schemes according to approved program
  Stage 1 Feasibility
  Stage 2 Design
  Stage 3 Construction
  Stage 4 Commissioning
  Stage 5 Post appraisal

- Monitor schemes at each stage as they are actioned and update program at least monthly
- Enter new schemes from strategies, action plans and Operator request
- Adjust new and phased scheme timescales to fit with desired expenditure profile and borrowing requirements
- Formally review program annually
- Report to interested parties (AMP/17)
- Continue to monitor and review at least monthly

Related Procedures

This procedure should be read in conjunction with the following procedures which are relevant to satisfactory completion of the process:

- AMP/11   Operator input to the CIP
- AMP/12   Investment identification and prioritization
- AMP/14   Costing
- AMP/16   Scheme appraisal

Function:	Asset Management		Ref.	AMP/16

Procedure:	Scheme appraisal

Author:	PWS	Manager:	SA

Created:	03/09/xx	Updated:	

Status:	Draft

Purpose and Scope

This procedure lays down the steps to be taken to appraise schemes in the Capital Investment program efficiently and effectively. It is relevant to all plant and pipeline schemes that are under the control of the asset owner.

Responsibility

The Deputy General Manager (Operations) is responsible for the production of this procedure, its updating and implementation. [CLIENT] will be responsible for ensuring that the steps contained are complied with.

Procedure

Stage 1 Scheme Appraisal

- Confirm existence of problems and the need for a scheme
- Check demand forecasts
- Identify potential solutions
- Produce revenue and capital costings for each alternative
- Appraise options using appropriate tools
  - discounted cash flow
  - cost benefit
  - criticality
  - profit and loss

- Choose preferred alternative
- Produce report (business case) with recommendation to set format
  - description
  - maps and plans
  - benefits
  - costs
  - timescales

- Submit for approval and confirm preferred solution
- Allocate priority and purpose codes
- Move scheme to Stage 2 in program

Post Appraisal (Stage 5)

- Carry out post appraisal of scheme to cover
  - costs
  - benefits
  - timescale

- File all records and update system maps etc.

Related Procedures

This procedure should be read in conjunction with the following procedures which are relevant to satisfactory completion of the process:

- AMP/12   Investment identification and prioritization
- AMP/14   Costing
- AMP/15   Investment programming
- AMP/19   Strategic development
- AMP/20   Demand forecasting

Function:	Asset Management	Ref.	AMP/19

Procedure:	Strategy development

Author:	PWS	Manager:	SA

Created:	04/09/xx	Updated:	

Status:	Draft

Purpose and Scope

This procedure lays down the steps to be taken for the orderly development of strategies. It may be applied in areas or functions where ALDAS requires a formal strategy to be developed.

Responsibility

The Deputy General Manager (Operations) is responsible for the production of this procedure, its updating and implementation. Use of this process is advisory only.

Procedure

- Review problem areas within City
- Determine those with the highest priority
- Break the problems down into functions and areas
- Bring in existing strategies and action plans
- Consider whether functions or areas are the best to use for each problem
- Draw up draft list of action plans to solve functional or area problems
- Group these together into either areas of functions - the groupings will form the basis of the strategies
- List the components of each grouping under a strategic heading
- Determine which actions are dependent upon the completion of others and order accordingly
- Examine which action plans will give the best results soonest
- Draw up an ordered schedule of the actions with draft timescales
- Consider the expertise and special technical requirements of the action plans
- Determine the expertise providers: contractors, consultants, in-house, researchers
- Estimate resource requirements for each of the action plans
- Consider the action plans in relation to total available resources and reschedule the draft program
- Finalize priorities and components of each strategic area under consideration
- Draw up reports and submit for approval
- Obtain approvals and amend program
- Draw up component contracts for survey, investigation and analysis

- Let contracts according to program
- Receive results of surveys, investigations and analysis
- Assess results and feed to Capital Program
- Proceed with Capital schemes
- Continue until problems solved

Related Procedures

This procedure should be read in conjunction with the following procedures which are relevant to satisfactory completion of the process:

- AMP/20   Demand forecasting
- AMP/21   Distribution Strategy
- AMP/22   Sewerage Strategy

Definitions

"Strategy"	A plan of action or series of plans for the conduct of a (military) campaign
"Plan of action" or action plan"	a small scale component of a strategy
"Function"	A set of related actions and plant for the provision of a related service e.g. water distribution or sewage treatment
"Area"	A discreet geographical area that can be defined according to a set criteria

| Function: | Asset Management | Ref. | AMP/20 |

| Procedure: | Demand forecasting |

| Author: | PWS | Manager: | SA |

| Created: | 04/09/xx | Updated: | |

| Status: | Draft |

Purpose and Scope

This procedure lays down the steps to be taken for the orderly forecasting of demand. It may be applied where [CLIENT] requires a formal water supply strategy to be developed.

Responsibility

The Deputy General Manager (Operations) is responsible for the production of this procedure, its updating and implementation. Use of this process is advisory only.

Procedure

- Identify command areas and horizon
- Obtain population statistics, forecasts and maps
- Obtain Town Planning information
- Obtain best existing usage figures for Domestic, metered and industrial components
- Set up metered domestic consumption trials (if not done)
- Request data and predictions from large industrial users
- Identify components of consumption and link to total usage
- Estimate 'unaccounted for water' including leakage from mains and private systems, free public use, and other losses
- Produce consumption figures with components for base year
- Confirm command area(s) and horizon
- Make assumptions, based on trials and planning information, of growth for domestic usage to produce profile of per capita consumption
- Use population forecasts to produce domestic consumption predictions
- Using factored responses from industry (according to confidence in data) produce prediction of industrial demand
- Produce prediction of commercial demand
- Add components for total demand prediction
- Estimate peaking factor

- Produce tables and graphs
- Circulate report with components and predictions for each command area
- Update annually

Sewage

- Based on the above map sewerage drainage areas (SDAs)
- Based on per capita usage estimate proportion returned to sewer
- Adjust for rainwater and groundwater entering system
- Calculate per capita then per dwelling flows based on average occupancy
- Estimate peaking factor
- Produce graphs and reports as above

Related Procedures

This procedure should be read in conjunction with the following procedures which are relevant to satisfactory completion of the process:

- AMP/19   Strategy development
- AMP/21   Distribution Strategy
- AMP/22   Sewerage Strategy

Definitions

"Strategy"	A plan of action or series of plans for the conduct of a (military) campaign
"Demand"	The daily customer requirement for the supply of potable water or the disposal of wastewater
"Command area"	The area under consideration forming a common water system, supplied for a single source or group of sources
"Horizon"	The limit of the timescales used in the predictions
"Unaccounted for water"	The difference between what is supplied at the sources and what reaches the customer and is paid for

Function:	Asset Management		Ref.	AMP/21

Procedure:	Distribution Strategy

Author:	PWS		Manager:	SA

Created:	04/09/xx		Updated:	

Status:	Draft

Purpose and Scope

This procedure lays down the steps to be taken for the orderly development of a Distribution Strategy. It may be applied where [CLIENT] requires a formal strategy to be developed.

Responsibility

The Deputy General Manager (Operations) is responsible for the production of this procedure, its updating and implementation. Use of this process is advisory only.

Procedure

- Confirm need for a Distribution Strategy
- Determine whether Greenfield or Rehabilitation

Greenfield Strategy

- Identify unserved area
- Confirm need to provide with piped system
- Consider alternatives
- Define area and draw up brief
- Allocate brief to designer
- Provide demand forecasts
- Designer surveys area, identifies resources, land requirements, treatment, reticulation and connection options
- Provisional report with outline proposals submitted and accepted
- Land requirements put in hand with Legal Dept.
- Following acceptance proceed with design, and tender documents
- Tenders let
- Construction
- Commissioning and handover to Operators

Rehabilitation Strategy

- Define overall boundary of study
- Examine records and determine deficiencies
- Plot strategic pipelines, problems and complications
- Split served area into discreet drainage areas (DMA's)
- Prioritize areas based on problems
- Organize survey and mapping program
- Survey metering points, and note deficiencies
- Organize programs of short term and permanent meter installations
- Organize pipe sampling and internal condition surveys, draft program
- Identify network analysis system and program
- Organize reservoir inspection program and drop tests
- Organize booster inspection and testing program
- Draw up coordinated rolling program of survey, mapping, inspections, testing and network analysis based on priorities
- Let analysis and reporting contract(s) to consultants
- Provide consultants with maps, LoS data, inspection / testing results, demand forecasts and reporting format
- Receive reports with analysis of existing system, growth predictions and outline recommendations for schemes
- Prioritize schemes and enter into Capital Program
- Monitor improvements and re-analyze when required

Related Procedures

This procedure should be read in conjunction with the following procedures which are relevant to satisfactory completion of the process:

- AMP/19   Strategy development
- AMP/20   Demand forecasting
- AMP/22   Sewerage Strategy

Definitions

"Strategy"   A plan of action or series of plans for the conduct of a (military) campaign

"DMA"   District Meter Area - an area served from a single point which has been identified and defined as the basic unit for study

"Greenfield"   Provision of new mains to a previously unserved area

"Rehabilitation"   Putting right the problems of an existing served area

Items to include in Leakage strategy

- 'Find and fix'
- Zones and DMA's
- Mains Records
- Burst records
- Meters and flow loggers
- calculation of water loss $U=S-(M+AP)$ where U is unaccounted for water, S is total supply, m is metered, P is population, A is Per capita in l/c/d
- night line surveys
- priority list of DMA's
- network analysis
- reservoir drop tests
- customer audits
- equipment
- pressure control

Function:	Asset Management		Ref.	AMP/22
Procedure:	Sewerage Strategy			
Author:	PWS		Manager:	SA
Created:	05/09/xx		Updated:	
Status:	Draft			

Purpose and Scope

This procedure lays down the steps to be taken for the orderly development of a Sewerage Strategy. It may be applied where the asset owner requires a formal strategy to be developed.

Responsibility

The Deputy General Manager (Operations) is responsible for the production of this procedure, its updating and implementation. Use of this process is advisory only.

Procedure

- Confirm need for a Sewerage Strategy
- Determine whether Greenfield or Rehabilitation

Greenfield Strategy

- Identify unsewered area
- Consider alternatives
- Confirm need to sewer
- Define area and draw up brief
- Allocate brief to designer
- Designer surveys area, identifies treatment or connection options
- Provisional report with outline proposals submitted and accepted
- Proceed with design, and tender documents
- Tenders let
- Construction
- Commissioning
- Handover then operation

Rehabilitation Strategy

- Define overall boundary of study
- Examine records and determine deficiencies
- Plot strategic pipelines, problems and complications
- Split sewered area into discreet drainage areas (SDAs)
- Prioritize areas based on problems
- Cost survey and mapping requirements and draft program
- Cost internal condition surveys and draft program
- Cost network analysis and program
- Draw up coordinated rolling program of survey, mapping, internal inspection and network analysis based on priorities
- Let survey and mapping contract(s) and receive results
- Let internal inspection (CCTV) contract(s) and receive results
- Let analysis and reporting contract(s) to consultants
- Provide consultants with maps, LoS data, internal inspection results and reporting format
- Receive reports with outline recommendations for schemes
- Prioritize schemes and enter into Capital Program
- Monitor improvements and re-analyze when required

Related Procedures

This procedure should be read in conjunction with the following procedures which are relevant to satisfactory completion of the process:

AMP/19	Strategy development
AMP/20	Demand forecasting
AMP/21	Distribution Strategy

Definitions

"Strategy"	A plan of action or series of plans for the conduct of a (military) campaign
"SDA"	Sewer Drainage Area - an area draining to a single point which has been identified and defined as the basic unit for study
"Greenfield"	Provision of new sewers to a previously unsewered area
"Rehabilitation"	Putting right the problems of an existing sewered area

Appendix 9
Sample AMS Manual

This sample of an AMS manual is provided to give guidance on the type of information that should be considered for inclusion. The purpose of producing a manual is to set down the structure, content and assumptions that have gone into compiling the AMS. It serves as a reminder to existing staff and as a guide to those taking up posts as a result of recruitment or staff changes. Being provided for guidance, it is not to be considered as definitive.

PLANT DATABASE - DATA DEFINITION

Field Name	Data Type	Description
SER NO	Number	Serial number created automatically
POP REF	Text	Plant or Process reference
NAME	Text	The name of the plant
ALT NAME	Text	Any alternative name for the plant
LOCATION	Text	The location of the plant
GRID REF	Text	The Grid References of the plant
USE	Text	The Service Code for the plant
MAP	Text	The Map Number where the plant is situated (1:25000 Series)
GROUP	Text	Group code appropriate to the type of plant e.g. Plant code, Well field, SDA
YR S BUILT	Date	Year the structure was built
YR M INST	Date	Year the mechanical and electrical was installed
AL M	Number	Asset Life of the Mechanical and electrical
AL S	Number	Asset life of Structure
LAND REF	Text	The reference of the land site used in the L & B database
FIN REF	Text	The site reference in the Financial system
OTH REF	Text	Other reference(s) relevant to the site
OP AREA	Text	Area code
ZONE	Text	The Service Zone
OP ST	Text	Operational Status (Code)

CRIT	Number	The Criticality Index
POP SERV	Number	The Population Served by the plant
CAP	Number	Capacity of the plant or process in Ml or Ml/d
T'PUT	Number	Throughput of the plant or process in Ml/d
UNITS	Number	Number of Units in the plant or process
MEAV-M	Currency	The Modern Equivalent Asset Value of the mechanical and electrical
MEAV-S	Currency	The Modern Equivalent Asset Value of the structure
PROC	Text	Process code (Major plants only) or Type Code (Minor plants)
CG-M	Number	Condition Grade of the mechanical and electrical
PG-M	Number	Performance Grade of the mechanical and electrical
CG-S	Number	Condition Grade of the structure
PG-S	Number	Performance Grade of the structure
RAL-M	Number	Remaining Asset Life of the mechanical and electrical
RAL-S	Number	Remaining Asset Life of the structure
REMARKS	Text	Remarks

Service Codes (USE Field)

Sewerage

STP	Sewage Treatment Plant
STS	Strategic Sewer
SPS	Sewage Pumping Station
MVP	Vehicles and Plant
MOE	Office Equipment
MCE	Communications Equipment
MST	Stores
MWS	Workshop Equipment
MLE	Laboratory Equipment
MCO	Computers

Type Codes (for Minor Plants)

Tubewells

VTP	Vertical Turbine Pump
SUB	Submersible Pump and Motor
OBW	Observation Well

Sewage Pumping Stations

VER	Vertical (dual well)
HOR	Horizontal Centrifugal
SUB	Submersible

Sewage Treatment

ASP	Activated Sludge
LAG	Lagoons
ALG	Aerated Lagoon
TRF	Trickling Filters
EAR	Extended Aeration

Operational Status Codes

AB	Abandoned, derelict
PM	Plant Missing
NW	Not Working
UR	Under Repair
PO	Part Operational
OP	Fully Operational
OB	Observation Well
NU	Not in use/Not being used

Data Collection Sheet

TREATMENT PLANT - PROCESS GRADES

Plant :

Ref # : STP

No	Process	Codes	CG - M	PG - M	CG - S	PG - S
0	Support Buildings	BLG				
1	Inlet PS	INL				
2	Screens	SCR				
3	Grit Removal	GRI				
4	Primary Settlement	PST				
5	Aeration	TRF ASP EAR				
6	Final Settlement	FST				
7	Tertiary	TER				
8	Sludge Treatment and Disposal	STD				
9	Other	GEN CAN PS				

Date: Collected By:

Operator's Name: Checked By:

Condition Grade Assessment (CG - S) Water Structures and Operational Buildings

Grade # 1 - Excellent
In virtually 'as new' condition. Requires no improvement work. Very well maintained and aesthetically pleasing.

Grade # 2 - Good
Sound condition with only minor appearance defects. Requires only minor maintenance like painting and repairs to fixtures.

Grade # 3 - Adequate
Some deterioration but not structural. Doors, windows defective; needs painting and rendering to damaged concrete. Only minor rusting of steel is visible which can be corrected.

Grade # 4 - Poor
Structural damage is evident. Cracks are visible. In some areas the concrete has failed and reinforcement is exposed. Roof may be leaking heavily. Severe rusting is prevalent. Complete rehabilitation is required.

Grade # 5 - Awful
Abandoned or not functioning due to structural defects. The structure could be unsafe. Requires total rehabilitation or reconstruction.

Condition Grade Assessment (CG - M) Mechanical and Electrical Equipment

Grade # 1 - Excellent
Electrically safe. Sound units generally in 'as new' condition. Asset adequate for the medium term with only routine maintenance.

Grade # 2 - Good
Electrically safe. In reasonable condition, showing superficial wear and tear; protective coatings still intact.

Grade # 3 - Adequate
electrically safe. All components functioning reasonably well. Early signs of significant (rather than superficial) wear and tear now starting to become apparent; corrosion becoming evident which is more than superficial. Minor failures have occurred.

Grade # 4 - Poor
Electrically safe. Effective life exceeded but still functioning. Repeated failures/breakdowns. Significant maintenance costs being incurred.

Grade # 5 - Awful
Electrically unsafe, or not working, or in extremely poor condition and frequently breaking down (in excess of 12 times per year).

Performance Grade Assessment (PG - S) Water Structures and Operational Buildings

The P.G assessment of structures is a measure of the ability of the structure to meet the level of service standards primarily in terms of pressure and flow.

Grade # 1 - Excellent
All customers are in receipt of a twenty-four hour supply with pressures in excess of 20 metres head of water. (Class 1 service)

Grade # 2 - Good
Customers receive 112 - 168 hours supply per week with pressures between 15 - 20 metres head of water. (Class 2 service)

Grade # 3 - Average
Customers receive 56 - 112 hours supply per week with pressures between 10 -20 metres head of water. (Class 3 service)

Grade # 4 - Poor
Customers receive 28 - 56 hours supply per week with the majority of customers receiving intermittent pressure of less than 10 metres head of water. (Class 4 service)

Grade # 5 - Awful
Customers receive less than 28 hours supply per week at intermittent pressures. This also includes customers that receive a truck borne supply or no water at all. (Class 5 service)

Performance Grade Assessment (PG - M) Mechanical and Electrical Equipment

The P.G assessment of equipment is the measure of the ability of the installed equipment to meet the level of service standards primarily in terms of pressure, flow and frequency of equipment failure.

Grade # 1 - Excellent
Units operating at 100% efficiency and standby is available. As a result all customers are in receipt of a 24 hour supply with pressures in excess of 20 metres head of water.

Grade # 2 - Good
Units operating at 80% efficiency and standby is available or units operating at 100 % efficiency but no standby is available. As a result customers receive 112 - 168 hours supply per week with pressures between 15 - 20 metres head of water.

Grade # 3 - Average
Units operating at 60% efficiency and no standby is available. As a result customers receive 56 - 112 hours supply per week with pressures between 10 - 20 metres head of water.

Grade # 4 - Poor
Units defective and operating at under 50% efficiency. As a result customers receive 26 -564 hours supply per week with pressures less than 10 metres head of water.

Grade # 5 - Awful

Units out of operation. Customers receive less than 28 hours supply per week at intermittent pressures this also includes customers who are in receipt of a truck borne supply.

PIPELINE DATABASE - DATA DEFINITION

FIELD NAME	DATA TYPE	DESCRIPTION
SER NO	Number	Serial Number
POP REF	Text	Pipeline Reference
U/S NODE	Text	Upstream Node
D/S NODE	Text	Downstream Node
FROM	Text	Location from which pipeline originates
TO	Text	Location at which pipeline terminates
NAME/LOCATION	Text	The Name or Location of the pipeline
MAP	Text	The Map Number where the pipeline is situated
LAND REF	Text	The reference of the land used by the L & B Dep.
FIN REF	Text	The reference used in ALCIE
OP ST	Text	Operational Status (Code)
FUNCT	Text	The Service Code for the pipeline
YR LD	Date	Year the pipeline was laid down
AL P	Number	Asset Life of the pipeline
POP SERV	Number	The Population Served by the pipeline
AREA DR	Number	The area of the land drained in ha (Sewers)
LENGTH	Number	Length in metres
SIZE	Number	The diameter of the pipe (I.D) in mm
MATERIAL	Text	Code for the material
JT TYPE	Text	Code for the Joint Type
PR RAT	Text	The Pressure Rating of the pipeline in metres head
GRAD	Text	The Gradient of the pipeline
ZONE	Text	The Service Zone
CRIT	Text	The Criticality Index
GROUP	Text	The Group Code applicable to the pipeline
OP AREA	Text	Area Code
CAP	Number	Capacity of the pipeline in Ml/d
T'PUT	Number	Throughput of the pipeline in Ml/d
CG - P	Number	Condition Grade of the pipeline
PG - P	Number	Performance Grade of the pipeline

S'FACE TYP	Text	The type of Surface over the pipeline
MEAV - P	Currency	The Modern Equivalent Asset Value per metre of the pipeline in $
RAL - P	Number	Remaining Asset Life of the pipeline (%)
MEAV TOT	Currency	Total Modern Equivalent asset value in $k
CAV	Currency	Current Asset Value of the pipeline $
REMARKS	Text	Remarks

Material Codes

CI	Cast Iron
AC	Asbestos Cement
DI	Ductile Iron
SI	Spun Iron
ST	Steel
GI	Galvanised Iron
PVC	uPVC
PE	MDPE/HDPE
CL	Clay
CO	Concrete
BR	Brick
OTH	Other than above (detail in "Remarks" column)
UK	Unknown
CM	Cement lining
BN	Bitumen lining
EP	Epoxy lining

Condition Grade Assessment

Sewers

Grade # 1- Excellent
Sewer is in as-new condition, routine maintenance only required.

Grade # 2 - Good
Pipeline subject only to minor surface and joint irregularities and not subject to collapse or blockage.

Grade # 3 - Adequate
Pipeline has surface and joint irregularities. Asset subject to very occasional failure.

Grade # 4 - Poor
Loss of cross section between 3 and 10%. Asset subject to regular failure.

Grade # 5 - Awful

Substantial loss of cross section e.g. more than 10 %. Asset subject to frequent extreme failure.

Performance Grade Assessment

Sewers

Grade # 1- Excellent

Hydraulically adequate at all flows. Capacity greater than current demand at all times.

Grade # 2 - Good

Hydraulically adequate at design flows. No adverse effects due to pipeline capacity or gradient.

Grade # 3 - Adequate

Pipeline provides reasonable level of service subject to backing up, resulting in restricted use, only occasionally.

Grade # 4 - Poor

Pipeline undersized or losing capacity due to deposits or structure resulting in poor service. May cause pollution at times.

Grade # 5 - Awful

Extreme hydraulic restriction under normal flows. Gross pollution problems even under normal operating conditions.